Those Were The Days
Lancashire
in the Forties, Fifties and Sixties

Ron Freethy

COUNTRYSIDE BOOKS
Newbury, Berkshire

COUNTRYSIDE BOOKS
3 Catherine Road
Newbury, Berkshire

To view our complete range of books,
please visit us at
www.countrysidebooks.co.uk

08641706
ISBN 1 85306 687 7

Designed by Roger Davis, K.D.P., Kingsclere
Produced through MRM Associates Ltd., Reading
Typeset by Techniset Typesetters, Newton-le-Willows
Printed by Woolnough Bookbinding Ltd., Irthlingborough

Contents

INTRODUCTION

When my publisher first suggested that I might like to write this book on Lancashire's history, concerned with this period, I felt a strange reaction.

Nobody likes to admit that they are knocking on a bit and the suggestion that I should compile a written and visual history of Lancashire between the years 1939 and 1969 brought me up with a start. I could remember the whole period very well and so I just had to accept that I am now history!

Would others, I wonder, feel the same and would there be sufficient interest to warrant even a small book? I need not have worried because my task has been to sift through and reply to almost 1,000 letters and look at an even greater number of photographs, advertisements and artefacts.

To appreciate how people felt in the years between 1939 and 1969 I decided to go back in time to the end of the First World War. Young men died in their tens of thousands and the so called 'Lancashire Pals' regiments lost almost a whole generation from the labour, leisure and pleasure markets. Yet Lancashire lasses gained equality (or almost so) and so in the 1920s it did indeed look as if Lancashire might have a generous slice of the 'Land fit for heroes to live in'.

Alas, the frivolous Twenties gave way to the hungry Thirties when economies and communities collapsed. People had nowt to spend on anything except food, and luxuries were only for the rich.

Just as recovery began the Second World War loomed and Lancashire's mills turned again and factories produced arms and ammunition. Although many young men paid the ultimate sacrifice the people learned to work again and self respect returned.

It is therefore fitting that this book of memories should begin with the war and the problems which followed immediately after it. Then came Harold Macmillan who told us that we had 'never had it so good' and up to a point he was right.

The National Health Service, an Education Act which although some called it elitist was far better than anything which had gone before, improvement in travel and leisure, fashion and fantasy shopping, buy now and pay later, pushed folk headlong into the Sixties.

There is no doubt that this period represented a changing age, and it has proved to be an enjoyable area of research for me.

Those Were The Days – Lancashire is an apt title indeed. I hope that I have managed to do justice to this time of enlightenment.

Ron Freethy

CHAPTER ONE
The War Years

F rom 1936 onwards it became obvious that war was coming. The annals of gearing up for war are groaning on hundreds of bookshelves and these give the impression of impending doom.

This was not the case, as many of my Lancashire correspondents have rightly indicated. Jobs were no longer under threat and the busy looms clattered away, foundries produced molten iron and steel essential for machinery, railway lines were forged or repaired and the canals also carried raw materials. The men in the Lancashire coal field burrowed into the bowels of the earth to provide the raw materials for the production of essential energy.

Lancashire's factories knew well how to produce cotton and they soon learned how to produce aircraft. This tradition of aeroplane construction has continued until the present day. The Canberra bomber, for example, was designed at the end of the war, first flew in 1949 and is still in service today.

There are two main reasons for the speedy evolution of the Lancashire aircraft industry. Firstly, there was an ever ready base of skilled engineers honed to a fine art by the cotton industry and these people proved easily adaptable to new techniques. Secondly, the new aircraft factories were some distance away from the Luftwaffe bases on the continent. Although they were not immune to bombing the Lancashire towns were not devastated as in the case of London, Coventry or Bristol. Although Liverpool and Manchester were bombed the mill towns were left largely alone and were able to get on with producing parts for aeroplanes and their assembly at places such as Chadderton near Oldham, Samlesbury near Blackburn and many others.

*Frank Whittle,
designer of the
Rolls-Royce jet engine.
(Rolls-Royce plc)*

It was at Chadderton, for example, that the Lancaster bomber was designed and many were built on the site. There is a plaque to the memory of the designer, Roy Chadwick, and in the visitors' centre at the factory is a photograph of him with Guy Gibson VC, the hero of the Dam Busters raid, pictured in front of a Lancaster.

There are many men and women who remember this period and as a result of my researches I met four men now in their eighties who had been part of a team working in an old mill in Clitheroe. Here they beavered away on the

*The Lancaster bomber, designed at Chadderton
and symbolic of Lancashire's 'war effort'.*

construction of a machine which looked like 'a collection of old milk churns'.

Fred Morley was the project designer for the Rolls-Royce jet engine pioneered by Frank Whittle. Allan Oddie was regarded as the finest draughtsman ever to work on jets. He was born at Waddington near Clitheroe and his skills were honed at Blackburn Technical College. By the age of 16 he was producing detailed working drawings from Whittle and Morley's sketches. Allan told me, 'There were thousands of first sketches and then detailed drawings for the fitters to work on. We then had a trial engine for Fred Morley to work with.'

'And for us to smash,' chimed in David Davies and Arthur Redsell, who were brought to Clitheroe and nearby Barnoldswick from Rolls-Royce in Derby to work on what was then a very secret project.

Arthur told me: 'What a lovely job we had. To take an engine and run it until it bust. Sounds like a schoolboy's dream doesn't it?' 'Ah,' interrupted Fred Morley, pretending to be fierce, 'but I always wanted to know where it bust and why!'

'I agree,' added David Davies, 'that was the difficult bit.' Out of the hard work and genius of this team emerged some of the most wonderful jet engines of the world, which continue to evolve around Barnoldswick until the present time.

As we sat discussing these memories, the four pioneers of aviation spoke together for the first time in more than 40 years of their Lancashire days when the first ear-splitting sounds began to issue from an old cotton mill.

Fred Morley had the last word. 'We were working at midnight and as we emerged from the workshop I was grabbed by the collar by an irate farmer. "Are you the bastard who's disturbing me cows?" he roared. "Don't you know there is a bloody war on?"'

The mercurial Fred laughed until he ached and added, 'It was too top secret to reply but I would like to have said, "Yes I do. Why don't you bugger off and let us get on with winning it"!'

It would be easy to fill the whole of a volume with memories such as this but the main thrust of this chapter is to discover how everyday Lancastrians coped with the war. Dry humour in this county is never far from the surface and this shines through as memories are recalled of air raid shelters, rationing,

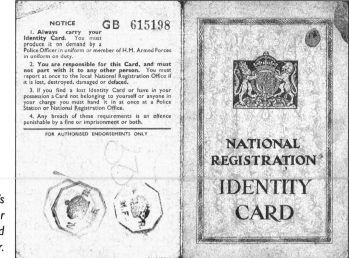

NOTICE   GB 615198

1. **Always carry your Identity Card.** You must produce it on demand by a Police Officer in uniform or member of H.M. Armed Forces in uniform on duty.

2. **You are responsible for this Card, and must not part with it to any other person.** You must report at once to the local National Registration Office if it is lost, destroyed, damaged or defaced.

3. If you find a lost Identity Card or have in your possession a Card not belonging to yourself or anyone in your charge you must hand it in at once at a Police Station or National Registration Office.

4. Any breach of these requirements is an offence punishable by a fine or imprisonment or both.

FOR AUTHORISED ENDORSEMENTS ONLY

NATIONAL REGISTRATION IDENTITY CARD

Jane Birchenough's Identity Card – one for every man, woman and child during the war.

entertainment, refugees and how families kept in touch with their menfolk around the battlefields of the world or endured the rigours of prisoner of war camps. And what about when the Yanks came?

'I remember Salford and district in the 1940s,' said 96 years young Marjorie Coates, 'and we were all sure that Hitler was coming by air. We had a communal shelter built of brick and concrete. We thought it was bomb-proof. In 1943 some youths hit it with a hammer and it fell down. Still we felt safe! There were also Anderson shelters which were dug in gardens and roofed over with corrugated iron and covered in soil and grass. Inside houses there were Morrison shelters which were like iron tables which you could crouch in. My children loved playing in ours and for several years after the war the Morrison shelter remained and when my husband came home on his old and noisy motor cycle our old cat headed straight for the shelter. Perhaps the cat had more brains than us.'

Brenda Hall of New Moston remembers the air raids. 'Perhaps one of my very earliest recollections is sitting next to my sister on the bottom stair while our mother fastened up our "siren suits" before taking us into the Anderson shelter which was just a few yards away from our back gate. During a night-time air raid we had been carried sleeping from our double bed and once the drowsiness wore off we had become boisterous in the shelter and the old married couple who lived next to us and shared the shelter were becoming

POST OFFICE SAVINGS BANK

£3% DEFENCE BONDS

BOND BOOK No. *143195*

The Postmaster General acknowledges with thanks your further purchase on the *20 Jan* 194 *1* of £ *5* . of the above Bonds.

Yours faithfully,

Leon Simon
Controller.

Exd. *W*

N.B.—If this communication (which is of NO VALUE to any one but the person to whom it is addressed) shows any alteration, or is inaccurate in any particular, it should be returned to The Controller, Post Office Savings Bank (Stock Branch), Harrogate, Yorkshire.

Mrs M Jacques
22 Newman St
Burnley
Lancs

S.B. 3 (Bond)

impatient at our childish antics. My mother, directing us to sit down and keep quiet pushed me onto a bench and my head hit the protruding edge of a sheet of corrugated iron and split open. I remember being carried out of the shelter, hearing the anti-aircraft guns and seeing flashes in the sky as I lay horizontal in my mother's arms.

We were encouraged to put our spare cash into Defence Bonds – the Jaques family (above) were typical of many. They even grew their own food on their allotment.

'On another occasion, round about the same time, my father was carrying me home to our house at night during an air raid and with my arms around his neck and my face close to his I felt safe. During the night if we heard the drone of an aeroplane we would become frightened and call out and our dad would come into our bed and we would immediately feel secure.'

Despite the great threat of war the young people got on with their lives, as a letter from Mabel Mustoe of Rochdale points out. Mabel remembers the year she reached 17.

'Come September 1939 war broke out with Germany and at the start we all feared for our lives; we imagined that bombs would drop on us every time the sirens went but we were lucky – it was the cities that suffered the worst of it. We became very complacent and stopped getting under the table or in the pantry when the sirens went. It got to be more of an adventure than anything, going out at night in the blackout, and it was black! Not a glimmer from any window and cars had hooded lights; not that there were many cars about as petrol was rationed. The insides of buses also had hooded lights and the conductor had a torch to see the money. We were never scared on the dark roads, even with no street lights – it really was very black. We wore luminous-paint lapel badges to stop us from bumping into each other.

'When I reached 18 in 1940 I applied for fire-watching at the factory where I worked; it was for one night a week and we got a couple of shillings and a free breakfast. We had camp beds in the bosses' office and an electric kettle. We amused ourselves on the typewriter and telephone etc. We were supposed to walk round the factory if the sirens went and look out for incendiary bombs which would have started fires; we were equipped with a stirrup pump and buckets of water. We put our pipe in the bucket and pumped like mad till the water came out of the hose; I swear it would have been easier to just chuck the bucket of water on the fire. Luckily we never had cause to use the thing in anger but we had lots of fun, although it was very eerie walking through the works with just a torch.

'We sailed through the war without much thought as to what was going on in "them foreign lands", we only saw newsreels in the cinema. If we were on a bus and the sirens went the driver would douse all the lights and usher us into the nearest shelter. Sometimes it would be two or three hours before the "all clear" sounded and Mum would be having fits wondering where I'd got to in

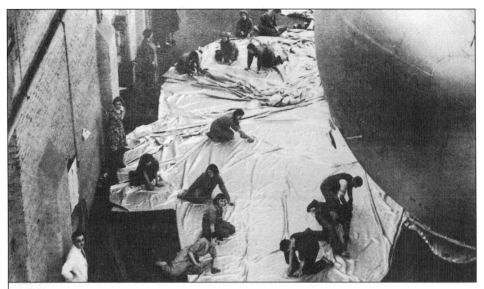

Helping to make the 'ugly flying elephants' – the essential barrage balloons – at the Dunlop rubber factory in Manchester.

The gas mask factory in Blackburn.

the early hours of the morning. We even had fun as a shelter full of people would start a sing-along to cover the drone of the planes heading for Manchester. If we decided to leave the shelter, before we got many yards an Air Raid Warden would usher us into another shelter so we couldn't win.'

Joyce Postlethwaite is proud of what she called with a grin, 'My war service. I loved it and I worked in the Dunlop rubber factory in Manchester. I used to laugh when I heard people describing barrage balloons as "ugly flying elephants". Some folk would not believe that I helped to make them.'

Mary Nield of Blackburn told me that 'as early as 1937 there was a gas mask factory in Garden Street, Blackburn and production reached fever pitch in 1939 and 1940. Who could forget the smell of rubber and the feeling of claustrophobia.'

J.B. Priestley, who apart from being a humorous novelist was a working journalist, described Blackburn during the war as 'Respiratoria'.

The newspapers, during 1940 and 1941, were full of stories of the devastation of bombing but on the whole Lancashire was left pretty well alone because the range of the bombers was at its limit. Bombs did, however, fall on Darwen and caused some deaths, whilst a single bomb fell in Burnley's Thompson's park and made headlines in the *Burnley Express*. George Tyson, now in his mid sixties, tells me that he walked around the bomb sites in Liverpool hunting for shrapnel and he still has one small piece in what he calls his 'memory box'.

On 20th June 1940 six bombs fell on Altham near Accrington killing three people, and three more were killed at Chatburn near Clitheroe on 30th October.

Preston got off quite lightly considering that the Germans knew that at Strand Road more than 3,000 bombers were being constructed. It was probably their failure to locate the Strand Road complex which led pilots to jettison bombs around textile towns in order to lighten the load and conserve fuel so they could reach their home base.

It soon became obvious that Britain could not survive without imported food but our reliance could be reduced by following the slogan 'Dig for Victory'. Here the Lancastrians did particularly well as the culture of the allotment and the miners' and millworkers' love of keeping racing pigeons stood their hungry families in good stead.

I have a personal memory as a four year old of learning that my father, who was an interested field naturalist serving in the RAF, was asked to locate and destroy the nests of peregrine falcons 'to help', as he put it, 'in the battle against Adolf'. It was thought that peregrines killed carrier pigeons and if we lost the war partisans would have to take to the hills and would not want messages disrupted by natural predators. At the end of the war I went with my father to see the nests which he had neglected to destroy because, as he rightly surmised, it would have made no difference whatever to the defence of the realm. These post-war revelations were directly responsible for my interest in natural history and subsequent career as a working ecologist.

21st October 1940. A German bomber dropped three bombs which landed in the town centre of Darwen.
The plane also machine gunned a Corporation bus and the death toll was seven.
Here the Fire Brigade are repairing the damage.

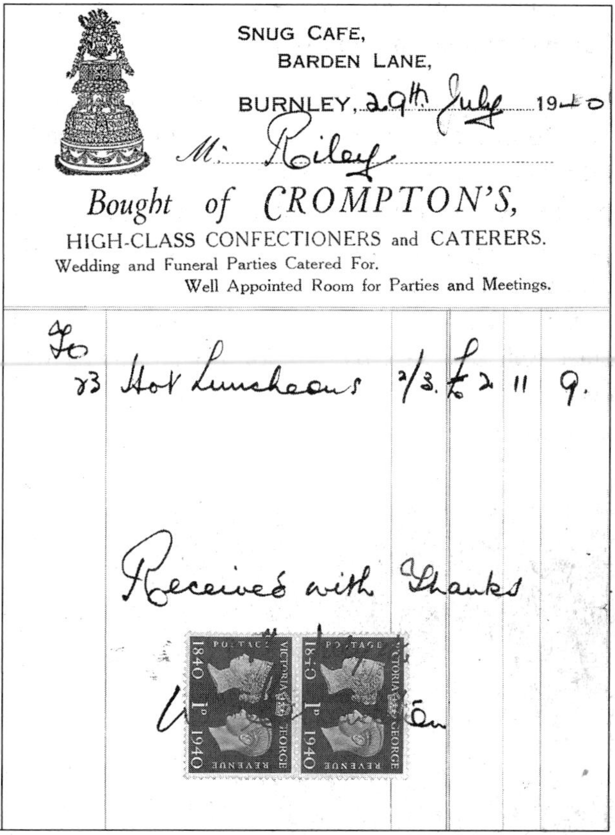

SNUG CAFE,
BARDEN LANE,
BURNLEY, 29th July 19⊥0

M: *Riley*

Bought of *CROMPTON'S*,

HIGH-CLASS CONFECTIONERS and CATERERS.
Wedding and Funeral Parties Catered For.
Well Appointed Room for Parties and Meetings.

£o

73 Hot Luncheons 2/3. £2 11 9.

Received with Thanks

*The bill for
the Jaques family's
funeral tea
in 1940.*

My father-in-law was a hard working cotton operative in Burnley and during the war he bred mice which 'were sent off for research, but we also bred rabbits, kept hens and jealously guarded our allotments and kept all seeds very carefully indeed. I don't think we ever went really hungry but the rations did not go very far.'

Actually it took time for wartime restrictions to begin to bite. Nobody thought that hostilities would last long. When Wilfred Jaques's mother died in 1940 the funeral tea was lavish enough to cost two shillings and threepence per head. The bill was receipted by a signature over stamps. These are also of interest because they celebrated the centenary of the penny post (1840-1940).

It is fascinating to look at a family ration book and then to pay a visit to a modern supermarket on what is described as a 'trolley filling trip'.

CLOTHING BOOK 1947 - 48 GENERAL CB 1/10

This book must not be used until the holder's name, full postal address and National Registration Number have been written below. Detach this book at once and keep it safely. It is your only means of buying clothing.

HOLDER'S NAME *MINNIE JAQUES*
(in BLOCK letters)

ADDRESS *22 NEWMAN St*
(in BLOCK letters) *BURNLEY*

HOLDER'S NATIONAL REGISTRATION No.
NFBO /222/ 2.

IF FOUND please take this book to any Food Office or Police Station

FOOD OFFICE CODE No.

N.W. 10.

THIS BOOK IS NUMBER *Y 769328*

HOLD Pages I—VIII in one hand and
TEAR ALONG THIS LINE

PAGE I

R.B.1 16

MINISTRY OF FOOD 1953-1954

SERIAL NO.

M of F

BP 996718

RATION BOOK

Surname *Jaques (Minnie* Initials

Address

IF FOUND RETURN TO ANY FOOD OFFICE

F.O. CODE No.

W-G, 3

Rationing went on well after the war – it was 1954 before the ration books could be at last forgotten.

In the late 1940s, for example, a man could have 13 ounces of meat, one and a half ounces of cheese, six ounces of butter and margarine, one ounce of cooking fat, two pints of milk and one egg. Not bad you might think for one day, but that was for a whole week!

I read this and then headed off to watch some teenagers enter a takeaway and consume two quarter-pounders with a topping of cheese and a mountain of French fries. And that was just a snack. How did a hard working man thrive on a 1940s diet? The answer is that most did not – they gave their ration to their children.

Sweets were also strictly rationed and I can remember being allowed my first box of chocolates. About a third of the box contained goodies whilst the rest of the spaces were filled with dried grass. This was not the work of a confidence trickster but due to the economy of sweet rationing.

Albert Gillings of Blackpool told me that when he returned home from a prisoner of war camp in Germany he had expected to eat steak and chips every

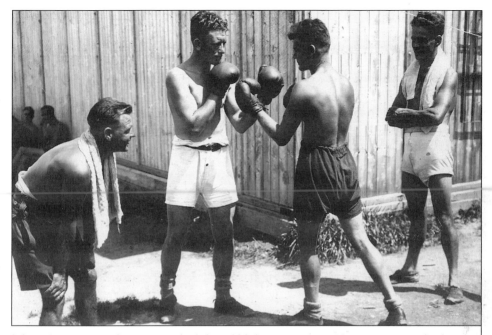

Life in the prisoner of war camps had the odd light moment — sparring practice and a home-produced pantomime passed the time for Albert Gillings at Stalag XVIII.

CINDERELLA

A PANTOMIME
PRESENTED BY
"THE EIGHTEEN DEES"
AT
STALAG (XVIII D)   DEC. 1941.

CHARACTERS IN ORDER OF APPEARANCE

CINDERELLA . . . . BILL HUTCHINGS
UGLY SISTERS {"CLARA" . . . . LEN SUTTON
             {"AGGIE" . . . . JOCK HUGHES
PAGE . . . . BASIL SMITH
FAIRY GODMOTHER . . . . FRED LANG
PRINCE CHARMING . . . . RAY MASTIN

ARRANGED AND PRODUCED BY F. D. (NIC) NICHOLS
ASSISTED IN PREPARATION OF BOOK L. (DAD) SUTTON
SECRETARY AND TREASURER L. (UNCLE) COWAN
ORCHESTRA UNDER THE DIRECTION OF
DENNIS WHITELEY (PIANO)
LEW STAFFORD (VIOLIN)   ARTHUR RILEY (TRUMPET)
DICK DAVIS (GUITAR)   ROY CROPPER (DRUMS)

SCENE 1.   KITCHEN
"SYMPATHY"   CINDERELLA
SCENE 2.   SISTERS BEDROOM
"TWO UGLY SISTERS"   THE SISTERS
SCENE 3.   KITCHEN
"WISHING"   CINDERELLA

10 MINUTES INTERVAL

SCENE 4,   BALLROOM
MEMORIES LIVE LONGER THAN DREAMS }PRINCE
LOVE WALKED IN   }CHARMING
SCENE 5.   STREET OUTSIDE KITCHEN
SCENE 6.   KITCHEN
STAY IN MY ARMS CINDERELLA } PRINCE
SWEET MYSTERY OF LIFE   } CHARMING

STAGE MANAGER . . . . . JACK. L. MASON
ASSISTANT STAGE MANA-
GER . . . . REG. COOK
LIGHTING . . . . J. L. MASON, FRED DENHAM
COSTUMES . . . . JOCK. CUMMINGS
SCENERY . . . . JIM WELCH
PROPS AND EFFECTS . . REG. COOK, TOM BAKER
PROMPTER . . . . JIM KALEY
VOICE . . . . GEORGE DUNNING

ACKNOWLEDGMENTS TO THE GERMAN CAMP STAFF
AND UNTEROFFIZIER W. LUDWIG FOR THEIR VALUABLE
COOPERATION

Blackpool Hotel and Boarding House Association

WE SERVE

WELCOME TO EX-PRISONERS OF WAR.

Members of the above Association request the pleasure of the company of

.... MR. A.E GILLINGS .... *and Lady friend*

on the occasion of a

Dinner and Social Evening

At R. H. O. Hills' Restaurant, Bank Hey Street, Blackpool,
On Wednesday, January 23rd, 1946.
Reception 6.15 p.m.   Dinner 6.45 p.m.

It will greatly help the catering arrangements if you will kindly
return the enclosed card not later than January 12th, 1946.

R. L. WIGHTMAN, President.
Councillor J. PARKER, Secretary.

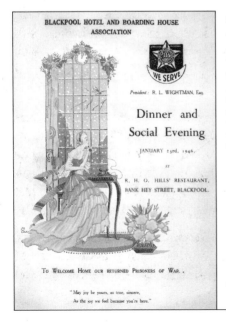

BLACKPOOL HOTEL AND BOARDING HOUSE
ASSOCIATION

WE SERVE

President : R. L. WIGHTMAN, Esq.

Dinner and
Social Evening

JANUARY 23rd, 1946.

AT

R. H. O. HILLS' RESTAURANT,
BANK HEY STREET, BLACKPOOL.

TO WELCOME HOME OUR RETURNED PRISONERS OF WAR.

"May joy be yours, as true, sincere,
As the joy we feel because you're here."

day. 'I got a rude awakening. The grub in the camp was lousy and it was great to be home. There was not a lot to eat until the early 1950s but the local hotels did us proud by organising "welcome home dinners" when some restrictions were lifted. I'd lived in Blackpool most of my working life and these dinners felt like as if we were guests of honour at the best hotels – but then I suppose we were!'

Mention of the word refugees or evacuees sets one thinking of sad, frightened

A 'welcome home dinner' for the POWs in 1946, attended by Albert Gillings.

children being packed off from the danger-threatened towns to safer places. Lancashire, however, played host to another group of evacuees. These were Channel Islanders, the wives and children being brought by ship and train to the mill towns. Here lasting friendships were forged, some of which persist to the present day. The evacuees found it hard to find work and Lancashire folk took pity by employing them as cleaners but they were really 'live in workers' sharing in the chores and contributing their meagre rations to the communal pot.

Minnie Jaques of Burnley kept a draper's shop and the Channel Islander Violet Machon did her cleaning and the children of both ladies enjoyed playing together. Marlene Jaques remembers that 'shortly after the war Violet Machon brought husband Fred and their new daughter over from Guernsey to visit all her new friends.

'In the May of 1948 we went to see them on the island and I can remember as if it was yesterday eating fish and chips and seafood as well as huge home-grown tomatoes. We went several times to the pictures and I can still remember everybody standing bolt upright and singing the National Anthem as if their life depended upon it. Well, I suppose it did because many folk were crying. We were there for the celebrations of Liberation Day with sports and a wonderful parade.'

One refugee who made his name was Jack Rosenthal, who hailed from Manchester but who settled in Colne during the war. He is now a well respected dramatist, well known for inspiring the early episodes of *Coronation Street*.

As the memories of war faded gradually, everybody wondered if politicians would make the same mess of peace as they did after 1918. 'It was,' as Wellington is supposed to have said after Waterloo, 'a close run thing'. But as the cold war and the nuclear threat fizzled out Britain warmed up and Lancashire learned to move from a war footing and the county's vast industrial energy was diverted to peaceful enterprises.

The aircraft industry used well tried construction techniques to produce 'prefabs', temporary houses which were put up to last ten years but some of which remain and are regarded by their owners as still functional and comfortable.

A final and on the whole happy reminder of Lancashire at War has to concern itself with the American Connection. The aviation historian Harry Holmes, a fount of knowledge and with a twinkle in his eye, told me, 'I've lost count of the number of times I've heard the phrase that Yanks are overpaid, over sexed and over here but I'll prove you wrong.'

Harry did just that and took me to see a party of American airmen and their English wives who married in the 1940s at the huge airbases at Warton near Blackpool and at Burtonwood near Warrington. Harry knew that I had worked for BBC local radio for many years and he introduced me to those involved in the American Forces Network, affectionately known as AFN.

'This radio station was a real part of Lancashire,' Sgt Alan Young told me, 'local folk could listen to the very best of American popular music including the Big Bands which later made such an impact especially in the 1950s. In 1943 one of our bombers was stuck by lightning and crashed on a school in Freckleton killing many children and also causing injuries. Some of us remember Bing Crosby visiting the injured and snuggling up to a little lass he sang *Don't Fence Me In*, but he found it impossible to hold back his tears.'

There is still a firm link between Freckleton and the Americans, and of course Warton is now used by BAe Systems for the research and development of the Eurofighter.

There can be no doubt that in Lancashire, and elsewhere in Britain, the Americans made friends and this point was well made by Beryl Collinge of Salford.

'On Good Friday 1944 American troops were billeted in all our homes for two weeks prior to the invasion of Europe. As they left another American came for two weeks and in his last few days he told us a lot of food had come with the troops to feed them whilst they were in the billets. We could have a frozen turkey or some beef. My mother chose a turkey but she had no experience of cooking frozen food and it was like shoe leather. Our neighbour across the road chose beef. We heard that the Yank shouted, "Here's your beef ma'am." She shouted downstairs, "Thanks, leave it on the kitchen table please." He then went out and when she came downstairs she screamed out loud. A whole side of beef was hanging across the kitchen table. Some of the neighbours helped to hack it apart later on when it thawed.

8th June, 1946

To-day, as we celebrate victory, I send this personal message to you and all other boys and girls at school. For you have shared in the hardships and dangers of a total war and you have shared no less in the triumph of the Allied Nations.

I know you will always feel proud to belong to a country which was capable of such supreme effort; proud, too, of parents and elder brothers and sisters who by their courage, endurance and enterprise brought victory. May these qualities be yours as you grow up and join in the common effort to establish among the nations of the world unity and peace.

George R.I.

Messages of thanks and of encouragement went out after the war to many who had participated in the 'Home Front', including the schoolchildren.

'So far as the cinema was concerned, I hated the smell of the sweet scented airspray which was used prior to letting the audience in to see the films. In 1942 my friend in the Wrens came home on leave and we went to the cinema. There were plenty of troops as well as civilians in the audience. The film got a bit confusing and people were murmuring to each other and then the screen went blank. As was customary the audience started to clap. The film restarted and we were even more confused. After about 30 minutes we saw scenes we had previously seen before the film stopped. The film finished 35 minutes later than was scheduled. All the way home people were discussing and arguing about what the film was really about and who did what etc. We came across a few Yanks and stopped to listen when one of them said, "I'm telling you fellas I know, I saw it back home and what happened was . . ." We didn't really get it sorted. It was common for films to break down but in this case an inexperienced operator had got the reels mixed up.

'So far as food was concerned one abiding memory was sponge cake made with liquid paraffin instead of cooking fat. We ate some but then supplies were restricted to pharmacists and were only available in small supply for medicinal purposes. I am not too sure but I think an announcement was made on the radio warning people not to use the oil for cooking as it could cause health problems.'

We were all sad when the Yanks went home but some still keep in touch with their Lancashire friends. This is, of course, made easier these days because it is so easy to fly.

As I neared the end of my researches for this book I spoke with Amy Baxter who told me, 'I was living in the States in 1944 and we also had rationing of food. All the good food was ear-marked for the boys who were fighting.'

There is a sad aviation contact concerning wartime Lancashire. Women aviators played a vital role by ferrying new aircraft from factories to operational bases. The famous Amy Johnson, who flew solo from Britain to Australia in May 1930, was working out of Lancashire on 5th January 1941. Amy ran out of fuel over the Thames estuary; her aircraft crashed and she was drowned.

It makes sense to conclude this chapter on the subject of aviation because we now take flight for granted, especially for holidays in the sun. Southport and Blackpool were offering pleasure flights as early as 1946 and from this simple beginning first the affluent and then the general public lifted their eyes to the heavens in search of a bright new world, which certainly shone out clearly by the end of the 1960s.

CHAPTER TWO
PEACE AND CIVIC EVENTS

I t certainly did not take long for the potential of aviation to stir the minds of Lancashire folk, as Bill Threlfall of Lytham, now in his nineties, pointed out.

'In the war I had helped to assemble aircraft at Samlesbury when I was living in Blackburn. The Wellingtons were there on the airfield and they were looked on as ours on their way to do battle with the enemy, but my mind was already working on the possibility of commercial flying. Once hostilities finished many ex-RAF pilots found it hard to adjust. The lucky ones got jobs providing pleasure flights from the flat hard sands of Blackpool and Southport. What was slow to catch on here was the passenger transport of the future. Folk still thought of ocean-going liners heading out from Liverpool rather than air liners from Manchester.'

Indeed, in the context of the new Millennium what the Lancastrians of 1946 viewed as an air liner now seems laughable. The Giro Aviation Company based at the Hesketh Park and Marine Drive areas of Southport boasted in 1946 that their De Havilland Fox Moth Air Liner was the height of luxury and gave certificates to those brave souls who cruised over the resort for a few minutes. Phyllis Jenkinson took to the air on 24th July 1946, the same year in which Wilfred Jaques first saw Blackpool from altitude. His great grandson now regularly commutes to Denmark! Such is progress.

What a thrill it would have been if one could have flown over Lancashire on the VE or VJ days of the 1940s or during the Coronation Year of 1953. These were the days of street parties which were developed to a fine art during the austere days when rationing still held Britain in its icy grip.

'It did not seem to be so bad at the time,' Ciss Gillings told me, 'we were all too glad to have our husbands back home. There was a spirit of togetherness because of the war and there developed a sort of 'Jacob's join'. We pooled our food and the authorities turned half a blind eye, if that's the right phrase. Everybody had a corner shop and the owners always found a bit extra for the party.'

Trestle tables, huge tablecloths, bunting and pianos, fiddles and tents

Passenger Certificate
This is to Certify № 168091

That..has flown in
a De Havilland Fox Moth Air Liner.

Pilot.

The Giro Aviation Co., of Southport have carried over 150,000 Aerial
Passengers during 21 years of post-war aviation.

WE RECOMMEND AND USE *Duckhams* AERO ENGINE OIL
ON ALL OUR AIRCRAFT.

An air liner? But at least in 1946 many Lancastrians were able to take to the skies for the first time, as Phyllis Jenkinson did over Southport.

A spendid VE Day bonfire at Cadley Causeway,
with Hermann Goering about to meet his fate.

The Coronation party at Peel, Blackpool was a great success. In the picture above – your very own cup, saucer and plate, complete with label!

sprouted like mushrooms in a warm autumn morning – everybody joined in sing-songs and couples cuddled, their inhibitions released by the thought of peace.

'At our VE street party we had a real treat,' Muriel Carson told me. 'We were living in Lancaster then. I'd be eight and my uncle sailed over to Southern Ireland from Heysham. There had been no war there and no rationing. My father and his mate collected money from everybody in the street and they brought back as much food as they could carry. There was beef sausages with proper meat in them and some strange yellow things called bananas. That was the first time that I had realised that bananas had skins on them. The only time I had heard of banana was when we went to eat in what were called British Restaurants. For pudding we were given bananas which were black and floated in thin watery custard.'

John Maitland worked in the docks at Liverpool and he recalled the VE Day celebrations and his street party in his home town of Bury. 'I had lots of friends in the Merchant Navy and they obtained lots of meat and fruit for me. I suppose these days you would call this stealing but these lads had a raw deal. Did you know that if a merchant seaman's vessel was sunk during the war their pay stopped because the owners agreed that they had actually jumped ship? No wonder they had a sense of relief when the war was over and almost all of them managed to get their hands on a few goodies for the party. My mate Rod Emery was an Australian serving in the Merchant fleet and he joined me at our street party. Between us we brought home a huge piece of pork. This was roasted outside and was my first experience of a barbecue. I have to say that I have never had a better one since and I'm now 93!'

The Coronation of Elizabeth II was a similarly happy occasion but the euphoria of 1945 and 1946 was now replaced by cautious optimism. Recovery had been slower than expected and rationing had lasted longer in Britain than in France.

Lancashire in 1953 was still a happy place, recalled Bob Hargreaves who was then living in Bolton. 'In 1953 we got pride back. A new young Queen was being crowned and watched by many on television, Hillary and Tenzing climbed Everest and two Lancashire teams reached the FA Cup Final at Wembley. That was the so called Matthews' final in which Blackpool beat Bolton. I was nearly 18 then and my girl and her parents helped to set up our street party. There were bonfires on the local hills and I was officially allowed to drink beer for the first time.'

Ciss Gillings also had memories of the Coronation party in Blackpool. 'We all saved up for weeks and I had the job of keeping the accounts and ordering the food. I'd love to be able to do something similar today but life has changed – people are now more insular and self-sufficient.' She then left me drinking tea whilst she rummaged about in her attic. She emerged triumphant. 'There,' she said, 'I've found it. That's my account book and a list of what we had to eat. We had a bonfire much as we did on November 5th but much more substantial. We roasted local potatoes in the hot embers and almost as if somebody had pressed a button, kitchen doors opened and the women emerged carrying hot pots, sausages, hot freshly baked bread and fried spam. I'll never forget spam. You could do anything with it. I expect you could have soled your shoes with it but we were too grateful to waste it. Others came out

INCOME	£ · s · d.	EXPENDITURE	£ · s · d.
Subscriptions, Donations, Whist Drives Etc.	102 · 4 · 4	Souvenirs	14 · 13 · 6
		Sports prize money	13 · 5 · 0
		E.P.N.S cups (Engr.)	4 · 8 · 0
Teas, sale of bread, cakes on June 6th	2 · 14 · 6	Catering	21 · 8 · 5
		Radio Van	6 · 10 · 0
Total	104 · 18 · 10	Hire of marquee	11 · 10 · 0
	98 · 9 · 10	Punch & Judy	3 · 3 · 0
Balance £	6 · 9 · 0	Magician	1 · 0 · 0
		Coaches	6 · 12 · 0
		Programmes	3 · 0 · 0
		Ice-cream, minerals	2 · 5 · 0
		Hire of tables, chairs & crockery	17 · 6
Balance equally divided and refunded to each household with children.		Tips to coach drivers	10 · 0
		Bunting & balloons	3 · 9 · 0
		L.D.P. paper (for tables)	8 · 9
		Sundries	5 · 9 · 8
		Total £	98 · 9 · 10

The Coronation Fund for Peel, Blackpool was meticulously kept by Ciss Gillings.

with treacle toffee and Jane Hughes who had married an American and had come "home" from the States for the celebrations brought lots of lovely chocolate. She had begun to use the word "candy" and could chew gum with the best of 'em. Jane's contribution was welcome but less welcome to some was her sister's offering. She was living in Bury and had brought black puddings and pigs' trotters!'

Despite these little luxuries food was hard to come by and people could still not eat as much as they wanted. 'Each person was given a plate of sandwiches prepared for them and labelled. It actually looked quite attractive and did add a personal touch.'

A feature of many of these street parties was the visit of the mayor, who must have been footsore at the end of the day, and also the National Anthem was sung with gusto. Brian Seward who celebrated the Coronation in Salford on his 15th birthday had his moment of glory.

'My grandmother had bought me a wind-up gramophone and I carried it to the party. The fragile 78 rpm records appeared by magic. I still have some of them to this day because kind neighbours added to my treat by each giving me one record from their collection. I was allowed to choose and I still have Bing Crosby's rendition of *Autumn Leaves* which had a South African label on it, whilst others I still play occasionally were George Formby's *When I'm Cleaning Windows* and Gracie Fields who sang a high pitched version of *Sally* in contrast to Paul Robeson's deep and sonorous tones of *Lula Lula Lula Bye Bye*. There were also three discs of the piano player Charlie Kunz who was, I think, blind. Then we all joined in. Our entertainment was simple. They tell us now that we had nowt in the Forties and Fifties. But nobody told us we had nowt and we enjoyed life, especially on those red letter days.'

Many of those people who corresponded with me during the gestation period of this book mentioned that street parties were only possible during the 1940s and early 1950s because the areas were clear of traffic. Marlene Jaques of Burnley remembers sledging down her front street during the frozen days of 1947. It was the onset of the private ownership of cars which changed the living patterns of people for ever.

The Whitsuntide Walks were one of Lancashire's traditions that seem to have largely disappeared as a religious festival, though a few thankfully remain.

Marlene has clear memories of being elected Rose Queen and leading the procession through the streets from the church.

Mrs E. Clarke of Wardle near Rochdale also remembers 'Whit Friday Walks with a service in the Town Hall Square and each church having a brass band leading and the Rose Queen and retinue following. Then came the church banners, guides, scouts, brownies and cubs with the Mothers' Union and members of the congregation at the back. Children held the banner strings and carried baskets of flowers. After the procession the congregations walked back to their own church. Then we went home to change our clothes which were always bought new for the occasion. In the afternoon we gathered at our Whit Friday field for fun and games and we were given a pie and bun with lemonade for the children and tea for the adults.'

The Whit Walks were typical of the Lancashire Cotton Districts, just like the Wakes Weeks holidays (see later chapters) and the county has one other

The Preston Guild restarted in 1952, to great enthusiam. This is Gordon Street.

unique form of celebration. This is the Preston Guild. These occur 'every Preston Guild' which does not mean never; the correct frequency is once every 20 years.

During the war years it must have seemed that the Preston Guild was an event passing into history. Guild year should have been 1942 but this was obviously cancelled. After the war a low key meeting was held in 1946 and the decision was made to hold the Guild in September 1952 after an absence of 30 years instead of the usual 20.

Then, as Pat Norman told me, the town really did let its hair down. 'VE Day, VJ Day and later the Coronation of 1953 were all wonderful but we shared these with the nation. The Guild was ours!'

Although the war had ended seven years previously there were some food items which were in short supply because rationing still applied. Pressure had to be exerted by National Government, with Lancashire's MPs backing the case for a relaxation due to the fact that the whole county loved Preston Guild.

Fireworks, eating, drinking, parades and plays took place. One of the most exciting was an outdoor performance of the *Mayflower's* historic journey to the Americas. A prominent part was dedicated to Miles Standish, a Chorley man who had been the soldier assigned to protect the settlers.

'Brass bands were everywhere, as they should be in Lancashire,' Eric Swinton of Preston told me, 'because every town and village had its band and so did most large companies and collieries. Among the more famous were Leyland Motors, Fodens, Wingate Temperance and CWS Manchester but there were lots of others. The most prestigious competition was held annually at Belle Vue which also had a zoo, a greyhound track and a Rugby League team.'

As travel became faster and cheaper during the 1960s some of the parochial fun disappeared from Lancashire's streets, villages, towns and cities. It is to the subject of travel that I turn in the next chapter.

CHAPTER THREE
GETTING AROUND

One of my earliest memories of a Lancashire mill town was the sound of clogs echoing on the cobbled setts of the streets leading down to the mills. Most folk lived within walking distance of their work but some travelled by bicycle, tram or perhaps by steam train.

This was still the case until well into the 1960s but even by 1939 there were some signs of change in transport patterns. The idea of a two or a three car family was an American dream and this affluent way of life was only to be found by going to the pictures. But almost everybody had a bike.

Cycling was a feature of the 1930s and this continued during and after the war, only fading as the affluent Sixties provided the relatively cheap acquisition of your very own car.

Lancashire is a hilly county but the struggle uphill was considered worth it in order to enjoy the carefree passage of the downhill run on a road still carrying little traffic.

'Lots of courting was done whilst working up a sweat pedalling through the Lancashire countryside,' wrote Jean Slater of Preston, 'and my friends knew we were going to be married when I turned down the offer of an engagement ring in favour of a tandem.'

Wilfred Jaques of Burnley had a cousin called Walter Gaunt who owned a cycle shop and therefore became aware of the technical improvements made in the years after the war.

'I think two of the main developments were better gears and stronger lights.

The gears made it easier for us folk of the hill country to climb steep slopes but what really sent us into the space age was the availability of affordable dynamos. Before that I can remember going out into the back yard and using a hammer to break lumps of carbide up into a white power. When water was dripped onto the carbide it produced acetylene gas which smelled awful and made your eyes water. When it was burned, though, it produced a dim light. This warned other people you were coming but it was not all that useful for folk travelling at speed. The acetylene lamp was useless in high winds because it just blew out. When I got my first dynamo the light seemed as bright as a wartime searchlight and it also charged up whilst you were moving. Cycling was wonderful but your first car was altogether different and just thinking of the names of the British cars of the 1950s is now a history lesson.

Wilf Jaques loved his car and it was carefully polished every weekend prior to the family jaunt into the countryside in search of pie and peas or fish and chips by the seaside or a substantial pub lunch, which also evolved during this period.

I remember my own early obsession with collecting car numbers and identifying each town by its registration letters. EO meant Barrow, then in Lancashire but now in Cumbria, BV was Blackburn, RN Blackpool, whilst the Burnley area had two identification plates, HG and CW.

Then there were the British Car Companies. There was Humber with its Snipe and Hawk, Austin, Morris, Jowetts which were handmade across the Pennines in Bradford and the impressive Jaguars made in Blackpool. There was the powerful Wolseley which the police often used, Triumph, Standard,

ANNE YORK'S motoring guide

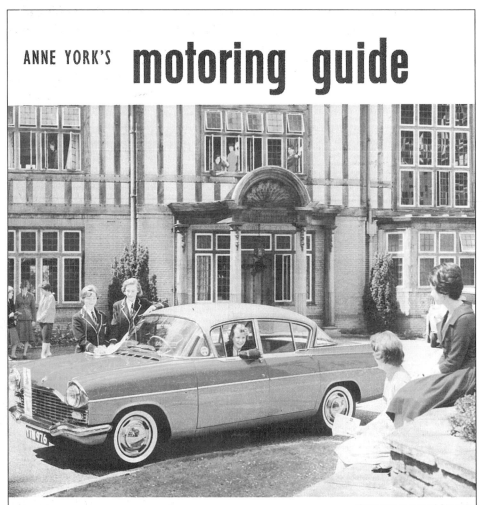

Photograph by Howard Symmons

OUR picture was taken outside Queenswood, one of the first schools to incorporate driving lessons into the curriculum of the Sixth Form at no extra charge. Here the girls taking lessons are gathered round the new Vauxhall Cresta. Parents are delighted that their daughters will be leaving school with this very useful extra accomplishment, and one of them has promised his lucky daughter a car of her own if she passes her test.

Instructors say that these young women make particularly apt pupils, and the results of their first driving tests suggest that professional driving lessons at an early age pay dividends. It is an idea we hope to see extended; for *new* drivers to be *better* drivers is one sure way of combating the toll of the roads during the years of motoring ahead.

Eight exciting pages of motoring news

Ford, and of course the Hillman stable. My first three cars were all Hillmans – a 1958 Minx, a 1963 Minx which cost £618 12s 9d new, and then there was the ill-fated Imp with the engine at the rear.

There were very few foreign cars unless you included Fords but even these were made in Britain under licence: the Ford Prefect and the Popular, which was just that, whilst those in search of an up-market vehicle went for a Cortina. There was not a BMW, Audi, Renault or Honda in sight. The British car and motor cycle were the envy of Europe. There were Nortons, BSAs, Royal Enfields and Triumphs. How things have changed.

Albert Gillings, when he returned to civvy street after being a driver in the army before his POW life in Germany, worked in a garage on Preston New Road, Blackpool and was the proud owner of a locally built Jaguar.

'It was really powerful,' he smiled, 'in a few minutes it could reach a speed of 75 miles an hour!' Albert then went on to extol the virtues of the all-purpose garage in the 1950s. 'These days,' he said, 'a car is repaired by removing the defective part and bolting on a spare. If the spare is not available then you have to wait until it is. What a car mechanic did in those days was to look at the broken part and make another to fit. You had to know all makes of car and you soon got to know their individual defects.'

John Dawson of Prestbury near Manchester remembers not so much the cars but the petrol.

'I remember how much easier it was when the garage where I was working changed from the old gravity-fed system to a power-pressured pump. What you had to do was to hand pump the fuel up into a glass bell which had marks down the side to indicate the number of gallons. When this reached the mark ordered by the customer the nozzle was inserted into the tank and a lever was operated. The fuel then fed down into the car's fuel tank by gravity. This took time and effort and the new automatic pumps meant customers usually did not have to queue and I was less tired when I got home from work. The idea of self-service petrol came much later.'

Having a car in the 1950s and early 1960s was not taken for granted as is the case today. Wilfred Jaques had to look after his Burnley-registered Vauxhall Cresta.

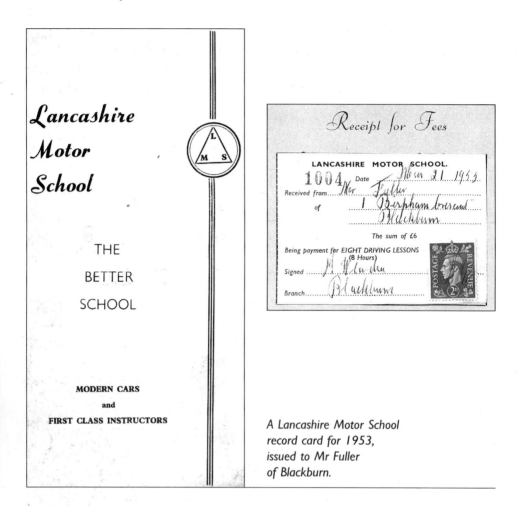

Lancashire Motor School

THE

BETTER

SCHOOL

MODERN CARS
and
FIRST CLASS INSTRUCTORS

A Lancashire Motor School record card for 1953, issued to Mr Fuller of Blackburn.

'Cars of this period tended to rust easily so they were not left out in the rain but were kept in a garage, which was not attached to the house but situated in prefabricated rows within walking distance. We had to insure the garage as well as the car and once inside the area the car had to be leathered dry. Starting in cold weather was a problem, especially because few of us drove to work and the car was left standing for several days. We used to place a small paraffin lamp under the sump to keep the car engine warm and dry. There were few people who left their cars in the street but they had little parking lights fitted to comply with the law. These lights were not much of a strain on the battery but they did cause some starting problems on occasions.'

As more and more people became car owners the demand for a specialist press accelerated and newsagents' shops had good sales of publications. The *Motor* magazine of 1948 anticipated this demand. It is fascinating to see an advert for the brand new Morris Minor, which has stood the test of time more than any model in the world.

Despite car ownership being the status symbol of the 1950s and 1960s, public transport was still the dominant form of locomotion which provided people with the means of getting to work and enjoying leisure and pleasure. Steam trains and coach trips homed in on the county's coastal resorts from the hard working towns of Lancashire.

Sunday rail excursions were an affordable treat and these only ceased as a result of the Beeching cuts which were such a controversial feature of the mid 1960s.

Mrs Brenda Hall of New Moston near Manchester really set my nostalgia buds bursting when she wrote:

'Even though we lived in terraced houses with no bathrooms and our

Wilf Jaques was the proud owner of a Vauxhall Cresta in the late 1950s.

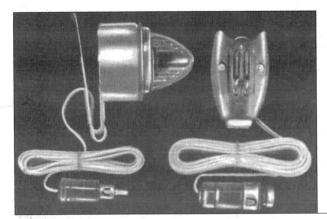

Parking lamps had to be fixed to cars if they were left in the street at night.

Three new Morris cars and two new Wolseley cars sweep on to the world stage. Like the Riley and M.G. 1½-litre models they have independent front wheel suspension. Steering Column Gearchange on the two larger Morrises and Wolseleys. Seats are within the wheelbase, to ensure smooth, shock-free riding; weight distribution is perfect. Streamlined for performance and economy. The mechanical excellence of the new models maintains the high standards of the individual members of the Nuffield Organization.

World Premiere

MORRIS · WOLSELEY · RILEY · M.G. · MORRIS-COMMERCIAL

PRESENTED BY THE NUFFIELD ORGANIZATION

Overseas business: NUFFIELD EXPORTS LTD., OXFORD and 41, PICCADILLY, W.I.

lavatories were outside in the backyard, we children did not feel deprived because there were fields all around us which were sometimes covered in dandelions. There was also a deep valley with a river running through it, which sometimes, after heavy rain, would become a raging torrent. Nearby were locomotive sheds and the beautiful steam trains were always present. My brother was in seventh heaven and always rushing off to get a closer look at a number or a name plate and checking it off in his train-spotter's book. Lying in bed I got to know what the weather was like before I even opened the curtains because I knew the

Prime Minister Harold Macmillan – 'You've never had it so good' – at Samlesbury Bridge on the very first motorway in Britain. The M6 was declared open in December 1958.

Carnforth Engine Shed in 1966, before it became a museum.

different sounds made by the trains' wheels in rain, snow or dry weather.'

After reading Brenda Hall's keen observations I now partly understand the modern day railway companies' excuse for delays on the line such as 'leaves' or 'the wrong sort of snow'.

Brenda went on to describe her exciting journeys to Blackpool in the 1950s by steam train which had 'sepia photographs of UK destinations above the moquette seats and I also remember the overhead racks made of strong netting. We were allowed, with care, to put our heads through the open window so that the wind blew our hair but as we approached a tunnel we would pull back into the compartment and detect the strange smell which was a feature of the underground stretches. It was said that drivers and firemen urinated in the fire and this made the steam odorous.'

The drivers were lucky because until the 1950s only the main-line trains had toilets, which could not be flushed whilst in the station. I myself remember one journey from Preston to the Lake District and busily consulting the timetable to see if I could make a dash for the station toilets at Lancaster. There was a five minute stop and I made it just in time.

The transition from steam trains to diesel and electric locomotives eventually led to the demise of the steam engine industry based at Horwich near Bolton and the old site is now within walking distance of the new Bolton Wanderers football stadium.

The period 1939 to 1969 also saw the transition from trams and trolley buses to double decker buses, many of which were built at the large works at Leyland. The history of Leyland buses is depicted in the town's impressive heavy vehicle museum. Some of these powerful buses are still in working order and make occasional pilgrimages to Blackpool from here or from a similar museum situated at Cheetham Hill near Manchester.

These buses replaced the trams, many of which were built by the English Electric Company which also built refrigerators. During the war the company first assembled and then designed aeroplanes, including the Canberra mentioned in chapter one. English Electric's heritage continues today under the banner of BAe Systems.

John Postlethwaite of Darwen describes himself as a bus and tram fanatic.

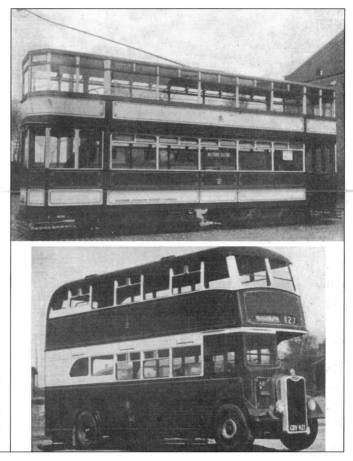

A covered double-deck tram at Blackburn in 1946 and Blackburn's up to date omnibus in 1954.

'Vehicle spotting can be boring these days,' he complained, 'because during the period of my interest each town operated its own transport system and its vehicles were painted different colours. If you stood outside Talbot Road bus station at Blackpool you could identify the visitors by the colour of the bus as well as by their accents.'

Nigel Phizaklea is only fanatical about trams and this is what has drawn him to Blackpool for a fortnight every year since 1949. 'You can only study the history of British trams in Blackpool because ever since 1895 the resort has kept faith with its trams. Manchester has at last realised its mistake and has reconstituted its tramway at great expense.'

Lancashire's towns' trams ceased to rattle along from the 1940s onwards. In Blackburn, for example, the last tram signed off at 11.30 am on 3rd September 1949!

So far in this chapter I have described transport for pleasure but also for work. There are further fascinating aspects of Lancashire's transport history during the period 1939-1969.

The Leeds and Liverpool Canal slices $127\frac{1}{4}$ miles between these cities and crosses the Pennines between Lancashire and Yorkshire. The Leeds and Liverpool has remained navigable since its final operational length in the 1820s. Its twisting course was designed to link the textile and coal towns such as Wigan, Chorley, Blackburn and Burnley. It is said that three 'C's made Lancashire's prosperity – these are cotton, coal and canals. The canal operated commercially until the 1960s.

'My father worked the barges between Burnley and Liverpool from the First World War until 1942 when I took over from him,' Tom Roberts told me from his retirement home in Morecambe. 'Life on a coal barge was a mucky job during loading and unloading and I can't remember going to school for more than a couple of weeks at a stretch. My mum taught me to read before I was five and I've read books all my life. I've read almost everything about Lancashire – including some of yours,' he told me with a mischievous grin. 'Moving a barge by horse was great because apart from the locks the beast knew more than I did and he even knew which pubs to stop at. We used to buy milk from a horse and cart near Hapton and the two working horses became great pals.'

These days the canal is purely a tourist attraction but it was a vital cog in Lancashire's industrial wheel until well into the 1940s and some barges made a good living until the 1960s although the horse gradually gave way to the diesel powered engine.

The change from real horse power to internal combustion mega-horsepower came gradually during this period and the transition was summarised succinctly by Mrs J.M. Britton of Eccles near Manchester who wrote: 'Up to the war there were few cars and lorries – horse and cart made most local deliveries and with petrol rationing that continued during the war. Our coal was delivered by that means up to 1955 and milk continued until 1957. Trams had disappeared and the rails been taken up late in the war – although I have happy memories of the trams along Kingsway to the Halle when they had to evacuate after the Manchester blitz, and later to Belle Vue from Eccles and to Farnworth. Barges still delivered coal and other supplies, again pulled by horses, all through the war and a little after. The leisure boating activity on the canals is comparatively recent.'

The last word on Lancashire's transport history has to concern itself with buses and coaches which remain popular, especially for football fans and 'mature citizens'! Many regret the passing of the Leyland buses which made the Lancashire town world famous. The Lancashire-based coach firms such as Ribble, Standerwick of Blackpool, Yelloways of Rochdale, Fishwicks of Preston and Maggie Smiths also of Rochdale have now all but faded into history.

Coach holidays can now be booked to local seaside resorts on an almost daily basis and increasingly since the 1960s trips to Europe have been regularly on offer.

CHAPTER FOUR
HAVING FUN

As I compiled the rough notes for this chapter I lost count of the number of correspondents who pointed out that people, during this period, made their own entertainment and did not wait to be told by television what they should enjoy. They also had to make an effort to travel to places of entertainment and the young could not 'wait for a parent to get the car out – most parents did not have a car and in any case there was a war on. We even managed to enjoy ourselves in the blackout,' remarked George Tyson, a Mancunian now living in Lancaster who then gave me a grin and a wink!

Mrs J.M. Britton of Eccles also makes reference to the young people's ability to ignore the bad things in the war. Mrs Britton worked for Metro-Vickers in Trafford Park where she became a dictaphone typist from the day she left school just after the start of the war. 'The blackout started almost immediately the war started but that did not keep us in! The Old Essians (school society) had a dramatic club and we did plays – the only snag was that people were called up as they reached 18 so that we had finally to give up – but not for a good while. We had a discussion group with a varied collection of people and that went on for a long time. There was also a music society that was very enterprising – we had a concert in the Town Hall with Solomon as the soloist – a notable occasion as the hall was packed beyond capacity – Solomon himself was handing out spare chairs to accommodate people on the platform! The Chief Fire Officer was there too, sitting with others on the window sills!

'The blackout did not incommode us at all – I only remember one truly dark night – the stars were so bright even when there was no moon. A girl friend and I walked with an older girl for miles talking – she guided our reading and discussed many things that were new to us. Boy friends were not an issue as they are nowadays – we had friends who were boys (a mixed grammar school meant that we could regard each other as persons not sex objects). We went

George Formby and his wife Beryl in 1963. Lancashire's own, George had been one of the most popular pre-war and wartime entertainers, and continued to enjoy a loyal following into the Sixties.

walking in the Peak District and later Youth Hostelling, and had a great time, both with the Old Essians at first and from work and the discussion group later.

'When London was bombed the opera and ballet companies came to Manchester for three week seasons at least twice a year and we saved up to go to as many as possible (back three rows of the Gods – one shilling). Sadlers Wells did all the operas in English so we really appreciated them. The ballet was enchanting and the Gilbert and Sullivan great fun. One of the men I typed for booked the seats on his day off in lieu for fire-watching. We also went to the Halle concerts at the Opera House and out along Kingsway and Belle Vue.'

On a freezing cold winter night in 1959 Dorothy Schofield of Littleborough

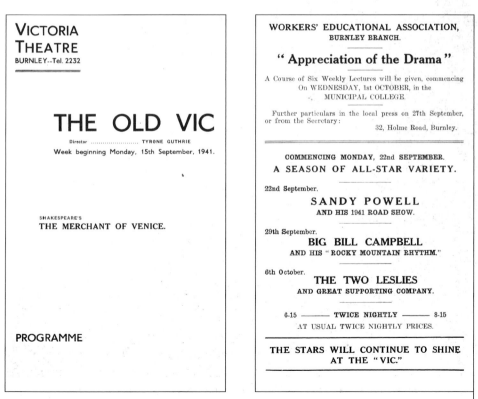

The Victoria Theatre ('The Vic'), Burnley offered a home to both the Old Vic and the Sadlers Wells Opera during the war, plus many well known variety acts.

remembers a coach trip to listen to Louis Armstrong and his jazz band. On the way home the coach broke down and she and her husband had to walk home with Dorothy in an advanced stage of pregnancy. They bred 'em tough in those days!

Of all the chapters in this book the present one is by far the most difficult, not to write but to condense into a compact section. A history of entertainment in Lancashire during this period would require several volumes. As usual, however, those who responded to my newspaper and radio station requests helped me to distil a strong brew of Lancashire's place in the history of British entertainment.

Let us first consider the decline and fall of live theatre which almost exactly covers the period between 1939 and 1969. Mrs Britton made the point that bombing in London caused the removal of world famous art forms to comparatively safer Lancashire towns and cities. My wife has strong theatre traditions in Burnley and she remembers Burnley's Victoria Theatre which opened in 1886 and which was affectionately known as the Vic. Actually the Old Vic Company performed here during the war and the theatre where Charlie Chaplin once performed was the base of the Sadlers Wells Ballet Company during hostilities. She performed there in pantomime and in 1955 as Adele in *Jane Eyre*. Also in 1955 the theatre closed after the performance of *Hobson's Choice* and so far as I know she was the last 'local' person to perform at the Vic. 'I seem to have been good at closing theatres in Burnley,' she said, 'because I was a member of Burnley Light Opera Society for some years. The Society was also a victim of the demise of live theatre. There was a continual struggle to find suitable theatrical accommodation. Its final "theatrical" base was at the Empire Theatre and this closed to make room for bingo in 1970.'

The last performance at the Empire was of *The Sound of Music* and as the sound of live theatre was suffocated by bingo the focus for this type of entertainment switched to Manchester and especially to Blackpool.

Blackpool theatres reached a peak of popularity from the late 1940s during the holiday season and the illuminations, which extend the season, right up until the late 1960s. Then foreign package tours began to divert the crowds to areas which boasted more reliable sunshine. In the winter Blackpool had (and still has) wonderful theatre as West End companies used the resort to try out potential hits on a more friendly northern audience. I have often spoken to friends of the Grand Theatre about these grand old days of post-war theatre.

The Grand was just that – it was one of the most attractive theatres in Europe and quite equal in decor to any in London. A restoration in the 1990s is a

The Grand Theatre, Blackpool is still one of the most attractive theatres in Europe.

The famous Tower Ballroom, Blackpool.

tangible reminder of the 1930s and 1940s when Lancashire folk queued for hours to obtain a ticket.

Whilst the theatre was badly hit by bingo the same cannot be said of pop music, both recorded and live. Some world famous groups including Gerry and the Pacemakers and the fabulous Quarrymen – who later changed their name to the Beatles – learned their performing arts in Lancashire's dance halls after taking their first tentative steps in their native Liverpool.

Learning to dance 'correctly' would soon be less important than it was in 1953!

Liverpool produced many of the new generation of pop bands, including the most famous of all –
the Beatles.

The Imperial Ballroom in Nelson, now demolished to make room for a car park, echoed to the huge beat of the big band and riotous rhythm of John, Paul, George and Ringo. Actually the original drummer was not Ringo but Pete Best who decided not to continue with the pop scene. He still lives in Liverpool. Even after Pete Best, Ringo's place was not secure. George Martin, the group's record producer, decided that Ringo needed 'more refinement' and brought in Alan White to drum on the recording of *Love Me Do*. Ringo, however, soon improved to become the bright and amazing star which he still is. The early Beatles hits, *Penny Lane* and *Strawberry Fields* are songs written about areas of Liverpool that are still attractive parts of the city today. And Ringo's voice rather than his drumming is now beloved by young children as

Many people bought the sheet music to songs in the Fifties, and Frankie Vaughan was always popular in his native Lancashire.

he is the narrator of the *Thomas the Tank Engine* stories.

Lancashire played an active part in the pop music of the Swinging Sixties and for a while the Hollies – a group from Manchester – were a real threat to the Beatles in the struggle to become the No 1 British group.

To most young folk of the 1940s, however, pop entertainment came from 78 rpm records and sheet music – it took a long time for the BBC to react to changing styles! Jill Saunders of Liverpool remembers 'going into my local record shop and asking to hear a Glenn Miller record before parting with my money. In those days you had to queue to enter a sound-proofed booth, close the doors and hear your record played. Some people tried to have several records played, especially if it was raining outside, but the shop assistants soon realised what was going on and put a stop to it. The shop got used to me because I always spent at least 2/6d (12½p) on a record and a piece of sheet music so they gave me plenty of time to choose. Many music shops were on two floors with instruments and sheet music on one floor and records and the booths on the other. I

loved Frankie Vaughan because he had Liverpool connections.'

The demise of sheet music did not occur suddenly but Brenda Hall of New Moston near Manchester identified the trend which began in the 1950s with the final eclipse coming in the early 1960s. 'At 15 years of age I thought that Doris Day was the tops. Even now, I do not think there has been a female singer to compare with her. Later the Everley Brothers' *Tears of a Clown* came out as a 45 rpm disc which I bought.'

So did I, Mrs Hall, and it was the first of its type that I ever bought. As I carried it home on a full bus I remember thinking that I hoped this format caught on because I did not have to worry about pushing through the crowded vehicle and breaking a delicate 78 rpm. Then came the 'Long Playing Records' which revolved at 33 rpm. I first bought the *Desert Song*, then *Flower Drum Song* and the *Pirates of Penzance*. All this happened whilst I was saving up for one of the new radiograms. It was as big as a sideboard and with a finely sprung playing arm which did not have needles which needed replacing regularly. There was a Gerrard turntable and a device which you turned in order to play 78 rpm, 45 rpm or 33 rpm. What luxury and there were 'no scratching sounds' during playing. All I can say in retrospect is that the phrase 'no scratching sounds' is a relative term.

For a while the new radiogram took over from radio itself and also I saved money for discs by not going to the pictures. The Ferguson was a popular make but it still cost more money than many could afford. The up-market folk could push the boat out in 1955 and go for a Dynatron. The standard version cost 52 guineas in an age when the average wage was in the order of £6 per week in Lancashire. Mind you, radiograms were not the be all and end all because potential girlfriends did not welcome lads who sat at home listening to recorded sound.

Lancashire had its share of stars of classical music. Kathleen Ferrier began her working life as a telephone operator in the Blackburn exchange before becoming a world famous contralto. Eddie Calvert cut his musical teeth in the brass bands of Preston before taking the record industry by storm as the Man with the Golden Trumpet who played *Oh My Papa* and other hits.

The 1950s and 1960s were the heyday of cinema when you had to queue to get in. Families went to first house and then on to the fish and chip shop.

Young people keen to meet friends of the opposite sex went first to the coffee bar (see chapter five) and then to the second house. During this period two features brought new horizons into the life of village children – the cinema and the increased use of public transport after the war. Mabel Mustoe of Rochdale remembers:

'When I got to about 12 years old Mum finally let me out of the village to go to the pictures on a Saturday afternoon, if I could coax the money out of Dad. We would get the train at the village station and get a return ticket to the next stop at Wardleworth. Just over the road was the Ceylon cinema known locally (as many others were in other parts of the country) as the "flea pit". There seems to have been hundreds of noisy kids in there but we all loved it.'

What films were Lancashire's favourites? The same as the rest of England I suspect but with two or three notable exceptions. One was *Whistle Down the Wind* which is now a black and white classic. Filmed mainly in Downham, it starred a young Hayley Mills and a group of local children, including Alan Barnes, who afterwards settled down to a normal and anonymous life in Lancashire.

My wife and I have a personal memory of this film in the sense that St Margaret's church, Burnley where we were married in 1962 was used as a location; soon afterwards the church was demolished and there is now a working men's club on the site.

Keith and Mary Hall of Downham also regularly re-run the film. Mary has lived most of her life in the cottage which was used as the post office. The film's premiere was at Burnley's Odeon Cinema, close to the canal. The stars and crew stayed at the newly constructed Kierby Hotel which still stands in the town centre (although its name changes frequently).

Still on the subject of Lancashire's classic film locations we have *Brief Encounter* which was shot around Carnforth station, whilst *Yanks* was filmed around Diggle, Delph and Dobcross, a trio of villages in the Saddleworth area. I always think that these villages sound more like a firm of solicitors than settlements!

Brenda Hall pointed out how important the cinema was to the young Lancastrians of the time:

The programme for the Royal Pavilion, Blackpool in 1952 – but whatever happened to 'Telekinema'?

'I still remember the thrill of sitting in a darkened cinema on a Friday night, feeling excited, watching Johnny Weismuller sitting astride an elephant in the jungle, and looking forward to Saturday night at either the Co-operative hall or Belle Vue dance hall where my sister and I would go with girl friends and stand on the edge of the dance floor, waiting for boys to come and claim us for a quick step, a fox-trot, a waltz and (something I never got the hang of) – the jive. There were always live bands, generally piano, double bass and wind instruments.'

A feature of all public entertainment locations was the pall of cigarette smoke which was highlighted by powerful lights. It is interesting to note that nobody linked cigarette smoking directly with lung cancer until 1946. Throughout the whole period covered by this book the non-smokers were in a minority and cigarette advertising was a major growth industry.

John Bottomley of Bolton wrote: 'I remember going to Preston railway station in 1948 as a 12 year old and combining my hobbies of collecting train numbers and cigarette packets. There were Woodbines, Senior Service, Capstan Full and Medium Strength, Black Cat, Camel, Gold Flake and hundreds of other brands.'

In the period between 1939 and 1969 the cinema was of real importance and the other vital area of entertainment was radio which reached a peak of popularity at this time.

Mrs Amy Catterall of Swinton remembered that, 'Our main entertainment was the wireless to which, along with my sister, I listened nearly all the time. Our favourite programmes were Valentine Dyal as the Man in Black, Paul Temple, Dick Barton and even Victor Sylvester who believe it or not taught ballroom dancing over the airwaves. I suppose this makes as much sense as Peter Brough doing his ventriloquist's act with his dummy Archie Andrews on radio! I also remember that my dad actually made our television in 1956. We all spent many evenings sorting out condensers which were colour coded whilst my dad soldered them into place. All the components were saved up for and bought separately. After many weeks the big moment arrived! Dad was up on the roof adjusting the aerial in response to our shouted instructions. At last we had a picture and sound. The first "performance" was a serial which was called the *Red Monkey*.'

Hayley Mills meeting the Mayor and Mayoress of Burnley

Jack Meadows of Southport pointed out to me in the course of a telephone conversation that a large number of the stars of radio were Lancashire folk. His impressive list included the Liverpool-born Tommy Handley of *ITMA* fame, Ted Ray and Arthur Askey, whilst non-Scousers included Al Read and Ken Platt. George Formby, Will Hay and Gracie Fields dominated the cinema.

My wife attributes her eventual career in dancing to the wireless. The popular *Children's Hour* featured a series called *Ballet Shoes* which led her to persuade her mother to allow her to go to dancing lessons. The dancing school she attended in turn provided much entertainment in Burnley by visiting most of the local church halls on Friday and Saturday nights giving dancing displays. The fact that Sadlers Wells was Burnley-based during the war was a boost to the town's dancing traditions.

Not just in Lancashire but throughout the whole of Britain the Coronation of Queen Elizabeth II in 1953 provided a massive boost for the sales of television sets. The early models had a small screen as Joyce Baker of Pendleton near Salford remembers.

'This nine inch screen was set in a great big polished wood cabinet which meant that the television was a major item of furniture which was kept lovingly polished. It had a magnifying glass slotted onto the screen.'

I can also remember the thrill I felt in the early Sixties when we bought our first 14 inch screen and then in the late 1960s we acquired a colour set which enabled us to watch Rugby League matches. To many Lancashire folk Rugby League is still a religion and is described in chapter 10.

It is not surprising that many remember the first episode of *Coronation Street* on 9th December 1960. Among those letting me 'in on her memories' was Joyce Baker. No wonder Joyce took a particular interest because Coronation Street did actually exist and was in Salford. When improvements led to the demolition of the so called 'slum' areas near to where the new Lowry Centre now stands, Coronation Street was dismantled brick by brick and re-assembled in the grounds of Granada Television Studios. In the days when I myself worked for Granada I often passed Doris Speed (Annie Walker), Bill Roach (Ken Barlow) and Pat Phoenix (Elsie Tanner) on their way to work.

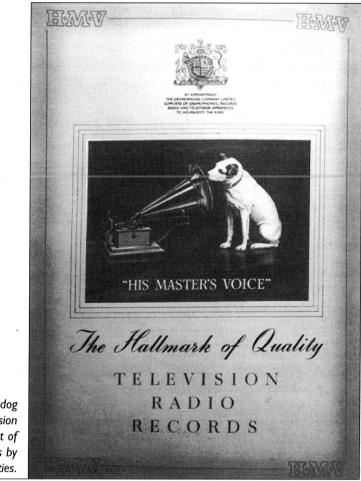

BY APPOINTMENT
THE GRAMOPHONE COMPANY LIMITED
SUPPLIERS OF GRAMOPHONES, RECORDS,
RADIO AND TELEVISION APPARATUS
TO HIS MAJESTY THE KING

"HIS MASTER'S VOICE"

The Hallmark of Quality

TELEVISION

RADIO

RECORDS

That familiar dog had added television to his list of attractions by the Sixties.

Whilst television eventually became an obsession to rival and later eclipse the cinema and radio, the young people of the 1950s and 1960s in particular continued to make approaches to the opposite sex by visiting such institutions as coffee bars and the concept of inebriated teenagers was unheard of.

Joyce Papworth of Rochdale wrote to me of the time of transition from radio through television and from buying direct to hiring.

'A popular form of entertainment was still the "wireless" then. We listened to programmes such as *Housewives Choice, Mrs Dale's Diary, The Archers* (an everyday story of country-folk), *Children's Favourites*, with "Uncle Mac" as the main presenter. At weekends *Two-Way Family Favourites* kept people in the Forces in touch with life at home and, of course, their loved ones. *In Town Tonight* was on most evenings and began with the sound of London traffic and "Big Ben". You could listen to good plays and serials (a science-fiction weekly programme starring a young David Jacobs being one of our favourites). Alvar Liddell was a famous broadcaster and read the news for us all during those days too. BBC wireless stations were known as the Home Service, the Light Programme and the Third Programme, and Radio Luxembourg was the first independent and we enjoyed them all.

'Radio remained popular long after television evolved and the *Goon Show* and *Billy Cotton's Bandshow* with its "Wakey Wakey" intro were both firm favourites. So was Cheerful Charlie Chester who always had an apt poem to keep his finger on the country's pulse:

> *Down in the Jungle*
> *Living in a Tent*
> *Better than a prefab –*
> *No Rent.*

'We got our first television set during the Fifties too, which was a "Rediffusion" model. Rediffusion became a big name in broadcasting on both radio and television. They introduced a system known as "wired vision" which meant they had quite a monopoly on the wiring and aerial installations (around the North West anyway). In effect, you rented all your TV programmes from them and, in return for your rental, they would undertake to repair any faults and renew your set for a more up-to-date model as and when they came out. Of course, the programmes were all in black and white then. Our family has hardly missed an episode of *Coronation Street* since it began in the early Sixties. Anyway, by the Eighties, there must have been too much competition and the name Rediffusion is now just a memory.

'Prior to 1971, British currency was "pounds, shilling and pence" (£ s d). Twelve pennies made a shilling, 20 shillings made a pound. Half a shilling was sixpence (or a "tanner" as it was called). There was the "half-crown" (or two shillings and sixpence) and the "crown" was five shillings (or "five bob"). A "florin" was worth two shillings. The red ten-shilling note was half of a pound and the pound itself was a note, not a coin. We had the £5 note, £10 note, but there were not too many £20 notes or £50 notes then, as money went a lot further. For example, you could buy a six-penn'orth (or 2½ pence) of chips and fish. You could ride all the way to town on the bus for 3d (1½p). Five pounds would easily buy a week's shopping then. A trip to the cinema would cost you something like two-and-six (12½p) in the best seats. How prices have spiralled since, eh!'

CHAPTER FIVE

COURTSHIP, CULTURE AND FASHION

I n addition to visiting the cinema or the dance hall, where did young people meet in the days when 'clubbing and pubbing' were either non existent or the sole domain of working men? During the 1950s and 1960s pub grub began to be on offer but where did the young 'uns congregate?

The answer was in the 'alcohol-free zones' of coffee bars and youth clubs, the latter being one of the most important institution of the 1950s. Two of the main items of furniture were the juke box which jangled away in one corner, whilst the coffee maker hissed and bubbled in the other. Both sported winking coloured lights and shining chrome.

In the late 1970s I bought a house which had once been a cafe. In a corner surrounded by rubbish I removed a partition. There I discovered a juke box still full of 45 rpm records. With excitement I dusted it, changed a plug and switched it on. Lights blinked and flashed and the sound of the Wurlitzer was a real blast from the past. My mind went back nearly 20 years in a flash.

I received a number of letters dealing with the coffee bar culture but no one caught the atmosphere better than Joyce Papworth of Rochdale. She remembers the hey-day of the San Remo coffee bar in Central Rochdale in the 1960s when the constraints of rationing were but a distant memory. Joyce wrote to me as if she actually was a coffee bar and I have to say that this unusual concept worked.

'I remember the day my owners opened the doors for business. They were so excited and yet apprehensive too. After all, they had ploughed most of their savings into converting me from the old-fashioned "Savoy" cafe, to provide a more up to date image. I knew they had little to worry about because, here on Drake Street, the position was perfect. Buses were dropping people off all day, some going to work in the other shops and small offices nearby and shoppers visiting the many and varied outlets the whole length of this busy, thriving, thoroughfare leading into the heart of Rochdale.

'So with my appealing decor, tasteful piped music, warm friendly atmosphere and varied menu, I didn't think it would be long before the proprietors began to see some reward for their hard work. You see, they were prepared to open all day and well into the evening, so there were plenty of customers – from shoppers wishing to take the weight off their feet and enjoy a mid-morning snack, to the lunchtime rush of workers from the variety of establishments nearby requiring take-away sandwiches and cartons of hot soup to enjoy by their rest room radiators, or to sit down inside here and treat themselves to a proper lunch with colleagues or friends for a complete change of scenery. I even remember the art college students from Fleece Street across the road. They were a weird looking lot with their long hair and sloppy jumpers but no trouble really – they got hungry too. Then there would be the afternoon tea people keeping themselves going until it was time to catch the bus home (hardly anyone drove cars yet) and they would be joined later by folk wanting to have their evening meal prior to a night out, either locally (seeing a film perhaps at nearby cinemas, or dancing at the Carlton Ballroom further up Drake Street) or maybe further afield. Oh yes, I became quite an important part of this northern mill town's central community.'

Mike Sumner of Blackburn is always a mine of information when it comes to the history and memorabilia of Lancashire in general and his home town in particular. Mike unearthed a trade catalogue of the 1960s catering for those setting up the new fangled coffee bars.

Amy Catterall of Swinton wrote: 'Growing up in our teenage years we had Milk Bars all over the place. These were teetotal establishments and in the late 1950s boasted juke boxes and these played rock and roll. We always went out as a group until people paired off and got married.'

The cinema and the dance hall were good ways for boys and girls to meet and

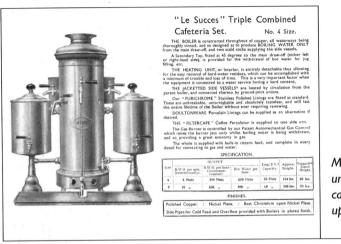

"Le Succes" Triple Combined Cafeteria Set. No. 4 Size.

THE BOILER is constructed throughout of copper, all waterways being thoroughly tinned, and so designed as to produce BOILING WATER ONLY from the main draw-off, and two scald cocks supplying the side vessels.

A Secondary Tap, fitted at 45 degrees to the main draw-off (either left or right-hand side), is provided for the withdrawal of hot water for jug filling, etc.

THE HEATING UNIT, or Interior, is entirely detachable thus allowing for the easy removal of hard-water residues, which can be accomplished with a minimum of trouble and loss of time. This is a very important factor when the equipment is connected to a water service having a hard content.

THE JACKETTED SIDE VESSELS* are heated by circulation from the parent boiler, and connected thereto by ground-joint unions.

Our "PURICHROME" Stainless Polished Linings are fitted as standard. These are unbreakable, untarnishable and absolutely tasteless, and will last the entire lifetime of the boiler without ever requiring renewing.

DOULTONWARE Porcelain Linings can be supplied as an alternative if desired.

THE "FILTERCAFE" Coffee Percolator is supplied to one side urn. The Gas Burner is controlled by our Patent Automechanical Gas Control which raises the burner jets only whilst boiling water is being withdrawn, and so providing a great economy in gas.

The whole is supplied with built-in cistern feed, and complete in every detail for connecting to gas and water.

SPECIFICATION.

Size	OUTPUT			Total S.V.* Capacity.	Approx. Weight.	Suggested Stand Height.
	B.W.O. per min. (intermittently).	B.W.O. per hour (continuous running).	Hot Water per hour.			
4	8 Pints	350 Pints	600 Pints	32 Pints	124 lbs.	26 ins.
5	10 ,,	450 ,,	800 ,,	60 ,,	156 lbs.	25 ins.

FINISHES.

Polished Copper. : Nickel Plate. : Best Chromium upon Nickel Plate.	
Side Pipes for Cold Feed and Overflow provided with Boilers in plated finish.	

Mike Sumner of Blackburn unearthed this 1960s trade catalogue for those setting up a coffee bar.

begin courting, but 'introductions' were best developed in coffee bars and youth clubs. To attract a partner, however, one had to look one's best and competition in the best sense of the word was intense.

The period between 1939 and 1969 saw major developments in terms of stockings and bras, both of these 'economic till busters' following the trend set in America and carried across the Atlantic by the GIs. In fact the word nylon comes from New York and London where the process was developed and by combining the names of the two cities, ie N.Y.Lon.

Before she died we had long conversations with my mother-in-law who once earned a good living by repairing ladders in silk and lisle stockings and later on by painstakingly repairing nylons. She had

A pair of these nylons would cost about half a working girl's weekly pay – no wonder nylons were painstakingly repaired!

Lycra was going to make life far more comfortable! The ad asks for details including 'Occupation' or 'Husband's, if married'.

extremely good eyesight. While these days the well dressed girl uses several pairs of tights in a week her 1940s to 1960s equivalent saved up hard to afford one pair of nylons and the sexy set of suspenders which held them up.

Drapers would travel to buy a pair of support nylons from a company in Millom in Cumberland which retailed around 1960 at 39s 6d – about half of a working girl's pay. No wonder that very wealthy looking ladies would come to Minnie Jaques's shop in Abel Street, Burnley to have their nylons repaired.

A 40-22-35 figure was the dream – until Twiggy appeared on the scene in the Sixties!

In 21 days your skin is transformed with SKINFARE

When you use Skinfare, the whole texture of your skin is transformed, and this natural miracle takes place in only 21 days. Neglected skin—even ageing skin—starts to take on the structure of young skin again.

Skinfare gives your skin a completely natural food, an essential food which becomes scarcer as a woman approaches the thirties. Skinfare does not contain any hormones. And the fullness, the smooth radiance of your beauty is re-created —naturally. You use Skinfare each night. There is absolutely nothing in the world so good for your skin.

ATKINSONS
Skinfare CREAM

9/6d · 16/- · 28/6d

At the other end, so to speak, the support bra began to take over from the literally straight-laced whalebone corset. The dominant colour of pre-war corsetry was usually pink and it was made of silk.

The idea of using artificial aids to alter the shape of the female body is not new and this continues to the present day. In the 1960s, however, ladies did not want to be thin; in 1963 Kurvon Laboratories based in Liverpool had developed a course of tablets to firm up the breasts and add 2 inches to the size! The ideal figure was to be 40-22-35! For a single threepenny stamp you could sample a tablet or two. A six-week course cost 30 shillings (£1.50) and a Mrs B. wrote glowingly to the company, 'After taking Kurvon tablets for only 6 weeks my bust is filling out – it is now 37 inches – an increase of 2 inches. I feel better too.' What present day weight watchers would feel about this I shudder to think.

The mothers of teenage girls from the mid 1950s onwards must have felt a little envious after their privations of the 1940s and early 1950s. Once the clothing coupons faded into history, nylons became available on request

Once wartime restrictions were gone, women wanted to recapture their lost years.

and cross-your-heart bras looked less and less like a suit of armour. Mums forgot about staining their legs with gravy browning and painting seams to resemble stockings and let their daughters go shopping for fashionable clothes. Proper lipstick replaced beetroot juice! Soon the ladies were being advised to paint their nails with Gala, colour their hair, and buy Boots No 7 make up.

Weren't liberty bodices sexy? – no. Weren't suspenders sexy? – yes. What about gingham skirts and stiff petticoats? Were they more scratchy than a gramophone needle? Probably!

What could the girls buy to wear over their nylons and bras? Mail order catalogues provided access to new fashions which could be paid for on the 'never-never' with Littlewoods of Liverpool taking the lead and their rivals Great Universal Stores (GUS) setting up a major location in Burnley.

Evelyn Wilson wrote, 'I worked for GUS when I left school and I'll tell you what was a real funny feeling. When a catalogue dropped on the mat and I could order the latest fashions I knew that one of my friends might process the order. There was a real problem if my friends ordered the same thing and we all went out looking alike.'

Mail order catalogues had the advantage of keeping people in touch with the latest fashions and provided an incentive to save up to have a shopping spree. To Lancashire folk this inevitably meant a journey by train or bus to Manchester at a time when the large department stores such as Kendal's, Lewis's and C&A were once more beginning to tap local, national and international markets.

Littlewoods led the way in catalogue shopping.

'At the age of 15,' wrote Margaret Hughes of Pendlebury near Manchester, 'I started work at one of the large stores in Manchester. At that time in the early 1950s the Deansgate area where I worked was full of bomb sites still waiting to be cleared after being badly damaged during the war.'

Female fashions will always predominate but the period between 1955 and 1969 saw something of a revolution in the clothes worn by men. Flared trousers typified the Sixties, Elvis Presley, Cliff Richard and the Beatles set trends in clothing and hair styles. There was some violence too as Mods battled with Rockers and, earlier, Teddy Boys did not always behave themselves. Cinemas in Burnley and other towns up and down the country had their seats damaged as the film starring Bill Haley and his Comets and called *Rock Around the Clock* resulted in loutish behaviour.

Despite the occasional lapse the behaviour patterns of the young were on the whole exemplary. Courtship invariably led to marriage with most brides then quite entitled to wear the virginal white. The relationship between the sexes was literally at arm's length.

Brenda Hall's courtship in the New Moston area of Manchester is typical: 'Around 1958 I, like many other young women, waved off my fiancé to do his

national service, he spending the majority of the two years in Hong Kong while I remained chastely at home collecting household things for my bottom drawer. In 1961 we were married at the same church where our parents had married, went to a very ordinary local pub for a ham salad, and welcomed friends to a party in the evening where a three-piece band played and everybody danced. Eighteen months later I gave birth to my first son in a small cottage hospital, with a little help from pethidine, and gas and air.

A cover girl for Men Only *who would have looked equally at home on a women's magazine.*

Two years later my second son was born at home in a two-up two-down house with no hot water supply. I stayed at home with my infant sons, as most mothers did in the Sixties, until they started school, when I secured temporary secretarial work during school hours.'

Mrs E. Clarke of Wardle near Rochdale remembers the innocence of the 1940s. She writes, 'I finished school as soon as I was 14. In 1946 I went to Blackpool for Rochdale's Wakes Week (the third week in August). This was the first time my friend Jane and I had been on holiday without an adult. On arriving we paid our landlady for our week's board, £2 15s. She was a nice motherly lady but strict about us being in early. We went dancing at the Tower Ballroom at 7 pm but had to leave at 9 pm and run back to the boarding house at the far end of Palatine Road to arrive by 9.30. One night, we had two boys with us and got back at 9 pm so we sat outside talking to the boys and at 9.25 the landlady came out and told us it was bedtime.

'Every day as we went on the prom we saw most of the people we knew, as Rochdalians flocked to Blackpool every August.

'The following year, 1947, I went to Heysham Towers Holiday Camp near Morecambe. All the girls were in the castle building and the boys were in chalets with a man seeing they did not get into mischief. If we went out with any boys we had to be in by 11 pm as the doors were locked then and a lady who we secretly called our jailer would give any late comers a really good telling off. Dancing ended at 10.30 pm.'

Later, after her marriage, Mrs Clarke was herself a Blackpool landlady and was thus quite aware of how moral behaviour declined from the 1960s.

Mrs D.M. Alber of Manchester has wonderful memories of courtship and marriage: 'I was 21 in 1939 and when the war started I was working in Manchester. My boyfriend and I often went to the cinema and to dances. We met in a Temperance Bar where we drank hot chocolate in the winter and lemonade in the summer. At home we listened to the radio or played the piano from the sheet music which was more popular than records at this time.

'Food was rationed of course and when we got married in 1943 we had saved up tins of food for months to prepare for our reception which was held at my aunt's house. I was not able to have a white wedding dress because we did not have enough clothing coupons. We could not have a wedding cake because the

essential ingredients were not available. Friends and family brought sheet music but we did have a wind-up gramophone with discs by Bing Crosby, Ella Fitzgerald and Frank Sinatra. When I had my daughter in 1949 I had no washing machine or vacuum cleaner and had to use an old-fashioned mangle and Ewbank carpet sweeper.' It is interesting to note that the Ewbank company was based in Accrington.

Dorothy Schofield getting wed in 1957 – and furnishing the new home for £221.

Dorothy Aitken provided lots of other fascinating details of 'making ends meet' during the war and just after. 'In 1949 food was still rationed but clothes had just become freely available. At the ante-natal clinic we were given orange juice and vitamins. We lived in a terraced house with no bathroom, the toilet being down the yard. Our tin bath was kept under the stairs and for some reason we used to sit in it during air raids. At this time I sometimes travelled to Sheffield by train but for security reasons all the station names had been removed. I was always scared of getting off at the wrong place and listened hard to hear the porter shouting the name of the station above the sound of the steam engine and clanking carriages.'

Until the 1960s and even beyond, the idea of saving herself for the wedding night appealed to almost every girl. Couples planning marriage at this time also saved their money and were not able to resort to credit. The idea of having a bottom drawer was not fanciful but a reality.

By the late 1960s weddings were becoming a major industry not least with regard to photography. Couples in the 1940s and 1950s made their vows and then headed for the photographer's studio. All couples were pushed into the identical pose and looked the same, and then came the 35 mm and sophisticated cameras which were affordable by the keen amateur. Flash photography made even more improvements in wedding photography which allowed each couple to celebrate their own individuality. My own wedding in 1962 showed these modern innovations whilst couples in the 1950s had much less room for manoeuvre.

Mrs D. Schofield's planning for her wedding in 1957 was not only meticulous but she and her husband kept details of purchases in the form of receipts. The result is that we now have a record of the prices paid for furniture and household repairs in Lancashire in the late 1950s. Her foresight makes me sad that I did not do the same. You do not think when you are young that all the luxuries which you save so hard to purchase are all too soon consigned to history.

The running of an efficient household also needs to be carefully recorded and this is the subject of the following chapter.

CHAPTER SIX

HOMEMAKING AND SHOPPING

The period 1939 to 1969 takes us from an almost Victorian attitude to running a house to the modern luxuries which we now take for granted. Many of the electric and gas cookers, washing machines, vacuum cleaners and televisions were actually made in Lancashire and there are many folk still alive and kicking who helped to manufacture these items and also used them in their own homes.

Lancashire was slower than most other counties to adopt and be able to afford innovations and the conversion from gas lighting to electricity was not complete in some homes until the mid 1960s.

Joyce Mitchell of Lancaster said, 'It was much easier to read when the electric came and I'm sure that we all had fewer headaches. We only had gas downstairs and until 1967 I went to bed carrying a candle. Because of electric light my man and I went to bed a lot later because we had plenty of light to read, play the radio and I could sew. Before mains electricity I remember taking big, heavy glass accumulators containing acid to be recharged. These powered the Cossor radio which we bought in 1938.'

Perhaps the most sought after luxury during this period was having an indoor flush toilet and a bath with running water. Following this in the list of priorities was a large and easy to clean kitchen whilst luxury furnishings and linen following the austerity of the war was not taken for granted until well into the 1970s.

Brenda Hall has a vivid memory of a way of life which disappeared only slowly during the 1960s: 'Imprinted on my mind from those times is the cold, blue linoleum on the bedroom floor across which I walked to trace with a finger the fern patterns in ice on the windows. Nobody had central-heating or double-glazed windows and though there was a cast-iron fireplace in the bedroom the only time a fire was lit there was when somebody was ill and had to stay in bed. Then, burning coals would be carried on a shovel from the living-room fire below.

'These of course, were pre-supermarket days, when nobody in our area had a car, when mothers walked us to and from school and took us to the Co-operative store where there were wide, wooden counters, and the assistants would add up the amounts for goods on long strips of paper, dampening the pencil leads between their lips periodically. My mother would arrive at the total before them, even though she was reading the figures upside down! Sugar and flour were ladled out of huge paper bags and great chunks of butter were gouged off yellow mountains. When the money was handed to the assistant the customer would quote their number and a tiny receipt would be

Gas lighting was still common in the Forties and Fifties.

torn off a foolscap sheet and at the end of the financial year members would receive a dividend, according to the amount they had spent, known, of course, as "divi".'

Margaret Hughes from Pendlebury wrote of her memories on the other side of the counter as she actually worked at the Co-op during the 1950s. 'Unlike today, our provisions were all delivered to us in bulk. One hundredweight of sugar, large tubs of butter, loose coffee, pepper and dried fruit. All these then had to be weighed out into individual bags, various wrappers and different coloured papers which enabled their contents to be quickly identified when things got busy. There were sides of bacon and hams which were wrapped in "cheese" cloths. There were no cold stores or counter fridges in those days and obviously no concept at all of sell-by dates.'

Some of the larger stores did not handle money or provide receipts. Customers' money and the assistants' reckoning were placed in a can which then whistled its way along wires to the accounts clerks in their office, usually above the shop.

What a joy to have a kitchen like this!

DALE PAUL

BRITAIN'S FINEST KITCHEN UNITS

I suppose it is fair to say that the Co-op shops which originated in Rochdale were the first supermarket-type establishments but until the 1970s the corner shop was an essential focus for everybody. Robert Ashworth of Rochdale remembers the Ellis shop in Jutland Avenue with the family living over the shop. 'These low-ceilinged premises offered goods ranging from bundles of firewood to butter from the tub skilfully shaped with wooden pats. After rationing ended we could plan our purchases once the Saturday pocket money arrived.'

Setting up a new home meant the chance to enjoy the benefits of modern furnishings.

In Lancashire there were specialist establishments including tripe shops which were typical throughout the county, whilst Bury's black puddings and Bolton's pigs' trotters attracted queues during the days when rationing ended and the butchers could do their jobs properly.

Locally produced confectionery products did a roaring trade in the 1950s and Eccles cakes, Goosnargh cakes, Everton mints and Uncle Joe's mintballs which were made in Wigan were in great demand. Little corner shops began to fill their shelves for the first time since the war and the children seeing these goodies were mesmerised.

There were certain items which even all the inclusive corner shop was not allowed to stock. Street traders were a vital part of early morning life in Lancashire and elsewhere throughout the period covered by this book. So milk, for example, which was delivered to the door, was one of these. Fish was another.

Jim Foster of Leigh remembers 'we waited for the milkman from around six in the morning, hearing his horses' hooves clattering over the stone setts in our streets. He had huge churns of milk fresh from the farm and from these he drew ladles holding a pint or a gill and which he measured out into our jug. We could pay with farthings, halfpennies, huge pennies, eight-sided threepenny bits, silver tanners, bobs or two bobs. We could if we liked pay once a week and this involved the use of half crowns or a red ten bob note. In the summer the milkman covered the containers with a piece of muslin weighted down with beads which were heavy enough to defy both the wind and the flies.'

Robert Ashworth of Rochdale remembered that other regular street traders operated from horse-drawn carts selling fruit and

Once homes had electricity, all manner of new appliances beckoned.

vegetables, and a fishmonger with a huge hand bell. His cart stank and had wooden flaps on the side to protect the ice-packed fish from the sun and the dust.

I can remember in the days before central heating that we all had 'a coil oil' and the horse, cart and muscular male carrier worked hard to keep each and every householder provided with coal. Until fairly recently women had to stay at home in order to keep the household running smoothly.

Apart from enjoying their food the Lancashire householders began to have an increased spending power. Furnishings now began to take on a new look and 'average' families soon began to look 'posh'. These new products changed the weekly routine as Margaret Hughes wrote: 'Before the days of washing machines Monday was always wash day. On Sunday nights the washing was put to soak in big wash tubs and shirt collars and cuffs soaped. Next morning the boiler was put on and the starch and "dolly blue" were mixed. Our first washing machine was a Hoover Twin Tub. One tub washed and the other had a motor which was a spinner. The washing, however, had to be physically lifted from one tub to the other.'

Gradually people's purchasing habits changed and I think that it is true to say that Lancashire was very slow to accept that buying 'on the never never', or 'on tic' or 'hire purchase' was not dishonest. As young people found work, courted, got married and began to raise children they found that they could obtain cars, washing machines, televisions and have solid, well designed furniture whenever they wished providing they calculated their finances carefully.

Masie Williamson of Southport remembers this period with a broad grin. 'My husband and I were both teachers and females were not encouraged to have children. Some authorities even preferred their lady teachers to be single. Obviously we both had good incomes compared to some and had good prospects because our salaries increased incrementally. This allowed us to run a Ford Prefect and to convert an old terrace house to our taste. "Our taste" in those days meant installing electricity, oil fired central heating (then the cheapest), a comfortable bathroom and fitted carpets standing on which was a three piece suite. I taught Domestic Science and my pride and joy was a Cannon cooker which I saw advertised on television by Philip Harben. He was at the forefront of television cookery along with the irascible Fanny Cradock

and Graham Kerr, also known as the Galloping Gourmet. In the late 1950s and throughout the 1960s I was an avid magazine shopper and as my father was a proud Lancastrian I felt obliged to buy from county-based firms. Our television had a Mullard tube which was made in Simonstone, Philips Electrical operated in Blackburn, whilst our Diana Cowpe candlewick bedspreads were produced at Hapton near Burnley. My kitchen equipment was Prestige or Skyline which were all made in Burnley.'

Masie Williamson went on to say that her grandparents felt that she and her husband were living in sin because everything they had was on credit. 'This

Diana Cowpe candlewick bedspreads were made at Hapton, near Burnley.

Prestige and Skyline were Lancashire products.

was not true and we paid our debts but the old folks of the 1960s thought that those who did not pay cash were courting disaster.

'When our children came along they loved visiting their grandmother who let them root about in cupboards where lots of household items resembled a museum. Their Grandma threw nothing away.'

This account is very similar to that remembered by Renée Blackburn of Colne who put her thoughts into verse.

Grandma's Cupboard

I opened the cupboard, inside there I'd find
A number of items of various kind.
Some wool meant for darning, in brown, blue and black,
A place on a shelf for Old Moore's Almanac.

Some pencils and pens and a bottle of ink,
A strong smelling liquid intended to drink,
The grandchildren came, always eager to share
The pear drops, striped humbugs and toffee in there.

The family bible, names written inside,
The family album with clasp on the side.
Our ancestors' photos in sepia hue,
An item for wash day, a new dolly blue.

Candles, some night lights, a gas mantle as well,
A dictionary's there to help folks to spell.
Marbles and tiddley winks for children to play,
When they visit Grandma on school's holiday.

Those who tried to sell expensive items on credit to those folk used to austerity were sure to have a sticky reception. The jokes about the vacuum cleaner salesman were particularly true in Lancashire between 1939 and 1969.

Beryl Collinge of Salford recalls: 'I saw my first electric vacuum cleaner when I was eight just before the war got going.

'At the time my mother who was born in 1902 used a small mechanical sweeper and of course every spring we all had to help beat the carpets with a

carpet beater. The carpets were dragged out and put across a washing line prior to beating. The vacuum cleaner was being demonstrated in Manchester's City Hall. The salesman put a large heap of dust on a carpet and swept it up with a handbrush and showed his audience a smallish pile of dust in the dustpan. Next he put a large pile of dust on the carpet and vacuumed it up. He then emptied the vac dustbag and showed us a large pile of dust. I thought it was wonderful and asked my mother to buy the vac. She walked away and said, "He had a lot of dust in that bag before he started." She did buy one a few years later, but she still saved up and bought it for cash.'

Emily Boardman of St Helens remembers a happy period of domesticity. 'From the late 1950s to the mid 1970s I made all my own clothes and those of the children. I remember one wonderful day when I saved up £15 (it took me nearly a year) and I set off early in the morning to Manchester. First I bought a portable Singer electric sewing machine which cost £9 17s 6d but I got it for £9 10s 0d by collecting it from the factory in Cheetham Hill. I spent the rest of the money on fabrics from the Manchester warehouses. When I got home our huge treadle sewing machine had vanished and in its place was a console television. Unknown to me my husband had been saving up as well.'

I am sure that Lancashire's reluctance to enter into hire purchase agreements and risk mortgages as opposed to paying rent was because of the ups and downs of the cotton industry. Wages could be good but there were long periods of recession and folk preferred to 'save their brass'.

As the 1940s gave way to the recovering Fifties and then to the booming Sixties there were more luxuries to tempt people.

'Once you could afford your own home,' said George Myers, 'you wanted to make it nice and comfortable.' Finding a house was not easy after the bomb damage of the war. Council houses gradually became available but not everybody welcomed the new luxury as Mabel Mustoe of Rochdale recalls. She was not happy moving into town. 'We moved into a council house but although the house was great, with a bathroom and toilet and a garden I wasn't happy. I missed my village life, my friends and the Chapel, and I went back there for quite a while to attend Sunday school.'

Some people, however, were less lucky in finding somewhere on their own to live without sharing with their family. Mrs J.M. Britton recalls: 'When I married in 1950 it was difficult to get accommodation – council houses were restricted to returning forces, or people with three or more children – my husband had such poor eyesight that he was not eligible for the forces – so we had to rent two rooms at first and when the first child arrived we borrowed the deposit for a house. We were desperately hard up paying off both the deposit and mortgage. There was no thought of working with a small child in those days, even with grandparents nearby to look after children. They were perhaps prepared to do the occasional evening baby minding.'

By the late 1950s grandparents began to look after children and this enabled women to work. This produced capital to fund a higher standard of living. What was typical of the period during and after the war was that everybody had to work hard in Britain. Lancashire was no exception as will be seen in the next chapter.

CHAPTER SEVEN

LANCASHIRE AT WORK AND PLAY

As cotton, coal mining and heavy industry declined, Lancashire over the period 1939-1969 gradually relinquished its title as the Cradle of the Industrial Revolution. However, there remained a work ethic within the county which still remembered the worrying days of the depression in the 1930s.

There was also a tradition of women working and yet still able to bring up their children properly without developing what was later defined as the latch key syndrome. There was a philosophy of work hard, play hard.

'In the 1950s the mills had their holiday funds which were taken directly from their wages,' Enid Wall of Blackburn told me. 'You could decide how much you wanted to save and then the week before the holidays began you were given your savings, and how rich we felt.'

Enid's brother John also had fond memories of this period because his father was at his busiest during the Wakes holidays of the 1920s and John carried on the family tradition. 'The origin of the Wakes holidays developed as a day off to attend the funeral (wake) of a mill owner, but once the seaside resorts of Lancashire got cracking each town had first a week and then a fortnight's annual holiday. During the holidays the mill boilers were doused and the huge tall chimneys were swept. That was my dad's first job and later I followed suit. Each town had a different holiday period and this meant that the resort towns could stagger their accommodation and the boiler and chimney sweeps like us could move from town to town.'

When I married in the early 1960s we did not go away during Burnley Wakes holiday. Each morning we looked out of the bedroom window and soon the visibility improved as the sooty atmospheres cleared.

In 1986 I wrote a history of those Wakes resorts and during its period of research I had several conversations with (now Dame) Thora Hird who herself told me of the joys of being a Lancashire entertainer earning a living both inside and outside the county. Thora, who was born in Morecambe, kindly wrote the foreword to that book.

'Although I have visited each town he writes about earlier in my life, after reading his book I now have a great urge to return to each place and wander about . . . with a copy of his book, opened and ready for me to refer to . . . Lovely Lytham and St Annes – Boisterous Blackpool – Thornton – Cleveleys – Fleetwood – Morecambe and Heysham, he writes about them all.'

I have also a personal recollection of Gracie Fields who I once met at her home on the Island of Capri. She told me of a 1938 memory when she travelled by train and car to Euxton near Chorley. She sang for the first time *The Biggest Aspidistra in the World* to celebrate the construction of the Royal Ordnance factory. In the following years, Gracie's song serenaded the workers at the factory during the war. 'We knew that this was the first time Gracie had sung the *Aspidistra*,' recalled Clara Westbury who worked at the site near Chorley. 'To us this was our signature tune and we always sang it after listening to *Workers Playtime* during the lunch break.'

Audrey Lees of Oldham has fond memories of holidays in Blackpool in the 1950s. 'We nearly always travelled by train. The track then followed the route now smothered beneath the M55 motorway. I also remember in the early 1950s going on an evening coach trip to the illuminations which were specially exciting because we had endured years of blackout and austerity.'

Brenda Hall of New Moston near Manchester remembers her early days of holidays. Manchester did not have a traditional town wakes holiday and 'People in my area did not seem to go on regular holidays as such but would go for days out to the seaside. Blackpool, of course, was the most usual destination, or they would go to visit relatives in other towns for a few days. In my family's case, my mother's grandmother, her aunts and uncles, lived in Dewsbury and we would go for short breaks there but the big, dark house in the unattractive town, where people spoke in a strange tongue, did not entice. However, when these same Yorkshire relatives came to stay with us in our Manchester home I found this very exciting and enjoyed all the gossip and laughter around me.

'Our first proper family holiday was one week in a Bispham boarding house: the party consisted of Dad, Mam, Myrna (14 years), Brenda (12 years) and Peter (7 years). This was approaching the affluent years when the two eldest daughters would start work.

'For a day out we took the long journey from Manchester to Blackpool sometimes on the bus, stopping about half way at a large pub called the Squirrel, which welcomed coach parties, rapidly pouring tea into thick, white cups, placed closely together in a square, the excess tea draining through the metal grille beneath. Mother would make and take sandwiches to be eaten on the beach, often filled with sliced tomato – and sand! Fish and chips would be consumed in Woolworth's cafeteria and from a window on the landing of the staircase one could ascertain if the tide was in. Once the sand was exposed we would hurriedly cross the promenade, Mum and Dad would get settled in their deck chairs, my sister and I would wriggle into our elasticated bathing suits and run into the sea.'

Ron Ormerod of Brierfield remembers the days when work and pleasure were almost inseparable. Oddies bakers, still famous in the East Lancashire area and operating from their base in Nelson, had regular staff outings to the seaside with the firm providing coach transport. This reached a peak in the 1940s.

*Oddies Cafe staff take a break, with the chef, the late Mr Bill Clements,
and the Oddies staff outing in the post-war years.*

Another firm in the same area was Althams which specialised in selling tea and coffee but their trips organised for employees became famous. From the 1950s onwards friends were also allowed to enjoy the trips. The company no longer sells tea or coffee but is a well respected Travel Agent with many outlets throughout the county. Another company with similar origins is Airtours which is now one of the largest travel companies in Europe. This still has a base in Rossendale.

In addition to being a supplier of textiles, Lancashire during the war was able to turn its hand to aircraft production based around Preston, Blackburn, Manchester and Blackpool. Locomotives and rolling stock were constructed at Horwich near Bolton, whilst Leyland was kept busy producing lorries.

The Lancashire coal fields operated literally at full steam during the period and on into the late 1960s. The Lancashire miners were a tough lot, and many living in the old coal towns have stories of the pits.

22nd March 1962 – the terrible day when an underground explosion at Hapton Valley Pit killed 19 men.

I remember during the 1960s sitting in the living room of my mother-in-law's drapery shop on Abel Street in Burnley and being regularly disturbed by vibrations caused by blasting at the Bank Hall mines which burrowed beneath the town.

I once spoke to the late John Nuttall who was a Burnley miner all his life. 'It wasn't a bad job if you made sure you got plenty of fresh air in your time off. Some lads kept pigeons, others went out with their whippets and greyhounds, but I got interested in bird watching. I learned to be a bird ringer and my hobby took me all over Britain but my most serious study was always based around East Lancashire. It was a lot more interesting than spending all night in the pub. It was a lot cheaper as well. It kept my mind fresh because mining was a very dangerous occupation.'

Bank Hall pit only closed in 1971 when it was judged to have become too dangerous to work. The East Lancashire mines were looked on in a different and more sensible light after the events of 22nd March 1962. It was a red letter – no, a black letter day – in the annals of Lancashire at work when an underground explosion at Hapton Valley Pit caused the deaths of 19 men. Marlene Jaques remembers this event very clearly. 'One of those killed was Gary Pickles who was in my class at school. Being killed at work seemed to be worse than being killed far away from home in a war.'

Marlene also has memories of early holidays and expressed the philosophy of Lancashire folk. 'Some people live to work but most people were not like that – they worked to live and to Lancashire folk they lived for holidays. As soon as the New Year's Eve celebrations were over they began to book holidays if they had not already said to their seaside resort landlady, "Same again for next year". My parents were more adventurous than most and caravanning was their hobby.'

These days caravanning is something of a luxury and a branch of Airtours called Eurosites will offer mobile homes or luxury tents all over Europe. What were the caravans like in the period 1949-1960? Actually they were nothing more than boxes on wheels, with lighting provided by gas with their delicate mantles always a problem for those who used 'sharp' matches in a careless manner.

There was usually a table between two long seats which had to be folded

A 'posh' caravan in the Fifties, perfect for the Jaques's family holidays.

down at night to produce a bed. 'In some of the larger vans,' wrote Bob Schofield, whose father looked after a caravan site near Morecambe during the 1950s, 'a wooden folded partition could divide the area into a second and more private bedroom. The really posh vans cost extra to hire and they had a simple cooker but many of the guests still brought their own primus stoves. In those days everybody carried water from a central tap and took the slops in the opposite direction to a midden. There was a privy block which stank a bit in hot weather and was always heaving with flies. There was also a shower block and sometimes, but not always, the hot water worked!'

It is, however, a question of what you were used to and a caravan holiday at the seaside was to many people a welcome change from guest houses with their often draconian rules and up-market hotels which were expensive but which still kept to strict meal times.

Many young men freed from the discipline of the services were keen to make

Loom making at Burnley, 1954.

their fortunes and some built caravans for themselves and their friends but obtaining the essential raw materials was always difficult.

Finding work just after the war was not a problem but folk had to be flexible. Lancashire's cotton was still in demand although much of the machinery was antiquated by American standards. Well into the 1960s, however, iron foundries were busy producing molten metal to be moulded into Lancashire looms and railway lines and steam locomotives were in great demand following the Nationalisation of the Railways in the late 1940s.

There was something of a problem as the aircraft industry shrank at the end of hostilities. Edward Berry of Preston wrote, 'Lancashire did better than most places because we were building Canberras which were in demand all over the world. I worked on this aeroplane and I also worked for a while at Chadderton, between Oldham and Manchester, on the Vulcan. These V bombers were our pride and the world's deterrent against the Russians during the Cold War. Lancashire had a stranglehold on aircraft design and construction at this time and I don't think we've ever lost it.'

Despite Lancashire's pride in aircraft technology there still had to be a rationalisation as armaments gave way to the production of luxury goods which were demanded from 1950 onwards.

'I worked for more than 30 years,' Sheila Compton told me, 'at Prestige, which was called Platers and Stampers. We made equipment for new fangled kitchens and the Skyline range was also made in Burnley. I had friends who worked at Bellings making gas fires and my husband worked at Mullards making television tubes. We all used to meet in the pub on Friday nights. We planned holidays together and all the works had schemes where you could buy goods for family and friends at factory prices.'

Every town in Lancashire and I suppose throughout the country had this type of factory as a result of the post war boom, 'but because of our engineering background the county attracted more industry,' writes John Cottam of Preston. 'We had Baxendales fires which even then was known as Baxi and my father was one of the first to buy a Bond Minicar.'

Bond Minicars were designed and made in Ribbleton on the outskirts of Preston. The first model hit the markets in 1950 and was simplicity itself. It was a three wheeler (one at the front and two at the back) and powered by a

125cc Villiers two-stroke engine. It had a roll back canvas hood and was therefore a true convertible. It did more than 100 miles to a gallon of petrol and was a two-seater, although there was 'room for two little 'uns in the back' said Jack Tyson of Lancaster who bought his Bond in 1951. 'We loved our Bond – to us it gave as much pleasure as 007 ever got from his Aston Martin.'

One aspect of Lancashire at Work which began in 1957 and which is still famous today relates to ERNIE, which began in St Annes and is now based in Blackpool. Minister Ernie Marples pressed the button to begin this Premium Bond-based prize fund, which many people wrongly referred to as a lottery. During the budget speech of 1957 the point was made: 'This is not gambling because the subscriber cannot lose. This is an encouragement to the practice of saving and thrift by those members of the community who are not attracted by the reward of interest but do respond to the incentive of chance.'

Many folk still have their first Premium Bonds and still live in hope as the Electronic Random Number Indicator selects the winning number under careful scrutiny. The Premium Bond office is still a major employer in the Fylde. I have spoken with the members of staff whose pleasant duty it is to tour Britain informing the winners of their prize. Most Lancashire folk, however, knew that very few people become rich overnight and that good times have to be earned.

Jack Tyson was an example of the work hard, play hard family ethic. Folk were prepared to give a good day's work and then spent their wages improving their home and widening their horizons by travel. In the 1950s most local papers produced articles and small books covering motoring runs within driving distance of their circulation area. This still goes on today and I have written this type of column in the *Lancashire Evening Telegraph* since 1969. Its title has changed over the years but 'Drive and Stroll' has always been the main thrust.

A fundamental change in a household's economy became obvious by the 1950s. In the 1930s finding enough money for food was a problem in many Lancashire households but in the 1950s all the family were prepared to work not to eat but to enjoy the luxuries of life.

Jean Simmons of Bolton writes: 'I began to keep a diary on Coronation Day in 1953 and I read through it the other day before writing to you. In the 1930s there was a pawn shop with its three-ball sign in almost every street. There is a note in the diary that the last "pop" shop in our area was closed down in 1961 and soon reopened as a furniture shop offering credit terms. That's what we called progress but even then not everybody was able to keep up with the payments.'

Young people also joined the labour market and were proud to help pay their way. Take Terence Hulme of Oldham for example: 'We were quite poor in the late 1940s, I can recall being given very little pocket money. At the age of 13 I could officially take my first job, that of delivering newspapers. But first you were required to pass a medical examination and then to obtain a local council work pass. Another drawback was that until you reached the age of 15 newspaper boys could not leave the shop until after 07.00 hours each morning. There were, however, no time restrictions in the evenings. My boss had been previously prosecuted for allowing a minor to leave the shop at 06.50 and so he was on the Education Officer's hit list. We knew that the Education Officer used to hide in the bushes and time us as we left with our bundle. Our payment for six days was 7s 6d (37 pence) for the evening round and 10s 6d (52 pence) for mornings. We also got bad weather payment with an extra 3d (one new pence) per day for heavy rain, snow or smog. During winter a battery torch was provided to read and check paper numbers because of the poor lighting provided by gas lamps.'

Terence Hulme went on to work in engineering but his life as a paper boy bridged the gap between childhood and serious work. It is the purpose of the next chapter to discover the life of Lancashire's children between 1939 and 1969.

CHAPTER EIGHT
A LANCASHIRE CHILDHOOD

The period 1939-1969 was a time of relative safety for children whose almost daily enjoyment was playing in the street. Lancashire youngsters loved snow and ice when the traditional cobbled streets were smoothed, especially by snow. The War Winter of 1940 and the Winter of Peace in 1947 were particularly white and very severe. Most Lancashire towns are constructed on hills and so the sloping streets enabled the brave (or foolhardy) to get up quite a speed on improvised sledges.

In the 1940s all streets could be used as play areas but by the 1970s motorists began to look upon playing children as a menace and parents did not allow their youngsters to take risks with traffic.

When it was wet children played indoors and Mabel Thorpe of Accrington wrote that 'we used to

Playing in the streets of Lancashire during the Fifties was safe. The coming of traffic and the family car destroyed the security and street games declined rapidly.

erect the wooden clothes horse and cover it with a sheet to make a tent. We could play for hours.' Most children could persuade their mother to lend them the clothes horse which was taken outside and sandwiches could add to the excitement of the picnic.

All children in this period integrated well within their immediate natural environment as Joyce Papworth of Milnrow in Rochdale wrote:

'It was 1950. I was two years old and my mother gave birth to my brother, Alan, in our local hospital (known as "Birch Hill"), a Victorian structure originally used as Rochdale's Workhouse. The war had ended and the work of renewal was beginning. At the time, our young family was living in cramped rented rooms with outside plumbing, as had many houses in those days. As local "Corporations" (as the Councils were then known) were building new housing estates, mum and dad put their names down and, because they had young growing children, were soon able to move onto the then largest Council estate in the country (known as "Kirkholt", meaning church amongst trees).

'When we became five, Alan and I began our school days (there was no such thing as "playgroups" then) at the infants' school in the heart of the estate, and a few years later, already having quite a good grounding in the three "Rs" by then (being able to do "double" writing already), we progressed to Kirkholt junior school (again a building within the estate). Each school was well within walking distance of home as, those days, cars were only for the better off. We continued our education for the next four years up until the then "Eleven Plus" examination, which determined whether or not you acquired a place at technical school, grammar school or secondary modern.

'We also were taught to swim during our time at junior school, most pupils obtaining a certificate for swimming at least a breadth of the pool after several trips by school bus each week to our nearest local baths which were situated in Castleton (one of Rochdale's outlying boroughs). These were the days when woollen swimming costumes were inclined to become heavy and drop off to everyone's embarrassment.

'One particular teacher at junior school (a Miss Wilkinson) had a motto which I've never forgotten – "If a job's worth doing, it's worth doing well"! In fact, I kept in touch with Miss Wilkinson, even after she retired to the Fylde coast, up

Children were quite happy to be organised in the 1950s as this church group near Blackpool clearly shows.

until recently when, inevitably, she must have passed away, because the Christmas cards stopped arriving.

'Although keen to learn, my brother and I just missed getting to technical school and were sent to Kirkholt Secondary Modern (again on the estate). An excellent establishment, we stayed there until we reached the age of 15 and had either to begin work or continue with our education if preferred. The school had its own huge playing fields for outdoor activities such as games, physical education and sports days. The teaching staff were excellent and we progressed well enough in our examinations to be offered "further education" at Rochdale's new Further Education College. I trained to become a shorthand typist, much in demand during the Sixties and Seventies and my brother took a course in painting and decorating (again a good skill to have).

'During this time, dad worked very hard as a cotton spinner at one of the local mills and mum kept house for us all until Alan and I were old enough to look after ourselves, when she would help out the family finances with part-time work as a shop assistant. There was no self-service in those days.

'During the Fifties not many working-class folk could afford to go abroad for their holidays. Mostly they got away as and when they could. Perhaps it would be a few days at Blackpool or, if you were lucky, a week or so "down south". We had an aunt and uncle who lived at the seaside, in Exmouth, near Exeter. They would find us bed and breakfast with local folk down there, as the four of us could not afford hotel prices when Alan and I were young. We travelled by coach initially, as Rochdale had its own coach company

(Yelloways) which became nationally known. I later became proud to work within that company, until its closure in the late Eighties.

'Coach travel for me was purgatory, as the motion of the vehicle plus excitement meant I vomited practically the whole of the journey. Mother tried all the "old wives' remedies" (including sitting me on brown paper and eating hard-boiled eggs) with no success. Thankfully, as I grew older, I grew out of my problem.

'Sometimes we did manage to afford rail travel. It was still the age of steam up until the late Sixties. Steam trains were wonderful, large and powerful, beautiful to behold. It was sad when Dr Beeching began closing railway stations and steam was replaced by diesel. These engines were much cleaner of course, but the magic was no longer there. Catering on British Rail in those days was quite basic, ie tea, coffee, sandwiches, chocolate bars – but one of the great favourites with people (me in particular) was the now famous Lyons Individual Fruit Pie which had holes in the top of the pastry, through which you could suck the fruit filling. Very good they were and no train journey for me was complete without one of those delicacies! They even came with their own boxes, so you were sure they had not been over-handled.

'Whilst my brother and I were growing up, we made friends amongst other children living nearby and at school, as most of the pupils were also growing up on Kirkholt estate. We would meet and play together, either around the nearby streets (which were practically traffic-free in the Fifties) or as we became older, we would wander down the nearby country lanes, where there was no fear of coming to any harm. We got lots of fresh air and exercise which was good for our growing bodies. No sedentary life for us playing computer games. We would play "Cowboys and Indians", mimicking the heroes of the silver screen, like Roy Rogers and Trigger, or the Lone Ranger and Tonto, his Indian sidekick. Rochdale had three cinemas, including the Kings and the Rialto (which was a beautiful Thirties-style building and very plush). People would form long queues right round the cinema waiting for the "first house" in the evening – the cinema queue being as entertaining as the film, if you stood and listened to the gossip going on around you – there was many a laugh to relieve the boredom until the doors opened. Right in the centre of Rochdale was the Regal which later became the ABC, one of the big names in cinema ownership.

'Boys had their own games, like collecting and swapping marbles; but us lasses would play hopscotch, dressing up, or skipping. Later on a new fad would be collecting and swapping "scraps" of many different designs and sizes (my particular favourites being cherubs).

'We all read comics, such as the *Beano*, *Dandy*, *Topper* and *Beezer* which we eagerly awaited each week. Like all children sweets were part of our childhood, even then (it's a miracle any of us kept our teeth). Items such as sherbet dips, or "Spanish" (which you could cut up and put into a bottle of water to make "spo", a type of mineral to drink on hot days). "Jubbleys" were a thick paper pyramid containing a lump of frozen fruit juice, to be sucked and licked as the ice melted. Lucky Bags became a craze too. The bags contained mixed sweets and, if you were lucky, a little toy of some kind.

'About once or twice a week, the ice-cream man would come round in this gaily-coloured van, announcing his arrival by playing "Westminster Chimes".

Popular children's annuals from 1961.

Children made up a rhyme to go with this, which was "Wall's Ice-cream, smells like Brylcreem", the Lord knows where this silly idea came from! We'd all run in and hope for a few coppers for a cornet or lolly. Ice-cream was made fairly locally then – ours was from a firm called Granelli's, in Heywood (the next town to us) and very good it was too. If you wished, you could have a squirt of "raspberry" juice on top of your ice-cream too, at no extra charge. Another street vendor was the Black Pea man, who rode round the streets on his bike with a large box of hot black peas. He would ring a handbell to announce his arrival and he must have done all right, because he kept coming round the estate for many years.

'In the late Fifties, Tupperware began the age of plastics in Britain which adults loved whilst the Hula Hoop was produced for children. This was a round plastic hoop (in different colours) and, after putting it over your head as far as your waist, was set spinning by gyrations of the hips, the idea being to keep it going as long as possible. Tupperware came out with the advent of fridges to keep food cool and fresh and consisted of different sized containers

The busy children's section of Burnley Central Library, though one young girl was clearly too tired to read.

(bowls or boxes) with air-tight lids, for separating various foods within the fridge for maximum hygiene. It proved very popular, as it could be washed frequently. Tupperware is still available today – and was marketed through the country's housewives, who earned commission on sales by holding "Tupperware Parties" for friends, relatives and/or colleagues, who could inspect the merchandise before placing orders with the hostess in the comfort of the home.'

Joyce Papworth's notes provided me with plenty of food for thought. The fact that most people – in particular young mothers – had no access to cars meant that great care was shown in the selection of the right pram. It had to be comfortable for the child and provide lots of space in which to carry the family shopping. The pram was often given by grandparents as a christening gift. A Silver Cross or a Wilson pram was the Rolls-Royce of the 1950s. The idea of carry cots and child seats in motor vehicles was only just evolving.

Jim Williamson of Bury adds his list of reading and he included the *Hotspur* and *Wizard*, 'which I think were printed in Manchester. Roy of the Rovers was my hero and so was Just William. Many Lancashire children read about William Brown, the posh lad from the South of England whose family had servants. Richmal Crompton who wrote the William books was a Lancashire lass.'

Indeed she was! Richmal Crompton was born in Bury and during the 1940s and 1950s William books were written at the rate of one or two per year. First editions are now much sought after collectors' items.

Reading comics and especially books was very much part of a Lancashire childhood and working mums and dads welcomed some teachers who stayed late after 'normal' school and supervised a homework hour. Local reference libraries also remained open until parents were home from work. Some towns, including Burnley, organised children's lectures and were visited by the likes of George Cansdale of London Zoo who brought some small animals with him, and Archbishop Huddlestone who preached that the Negroes in South Africa should be treated with more respect. He was a lifelong supporter of Nelson Mandela.

These homework periods and lectures were more important during the winter because 'playing out' was usually more attractive in the warm summer

The Burnley Police Youth Club camp in 1943 (top) and the club boxing team in the late 1940s. Most youngsters joined a club of some sort.

evenings. These idyllic days were remembered by Brenda Hall of New Moston.

'Skipping rope games were a great favourite with little girls as was throwing two balls at brick walls, catching and bouncing them on the rebound. The boys liked kicking balls about and we girls would join them sometimes in cricket games with the wickets drawn in chalk on gable ends. Boys too would form gangs and wage war by throwing stones at each other. "Black and White Rabbit", or knocking at doors and running away was considered to be exciting. This game was reserved for wintertime when we played outdoors after dark. Candles would be carried around in jam jars suspended on string. October and November were the months when "logging" was the essential pastime: we had to collect a lot of wood for the communal bonfire when adults got involved, carrying benches to be placed at a safe distance from the hot ashes, placing big potatoes in the fire to be eaten later with salt, the better-off parents producing treacle toffee for distribution to the children. Dandelion and burdock drink was the usual accompaniment although American Cream Soda was considered by some as a rather daring liquid.

'This was the era when back doors were always on the latch, never bolted and when neighbours knocked and walked in. Hopscotch, pitch-weighted arrows

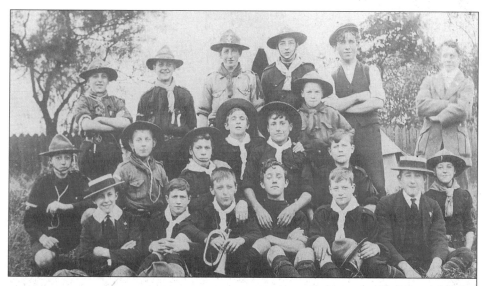

Scout camp at Burnley in 1944.

slung with string, rounders, netball, spinning tops, simply running for the sheer joy of it – so many distractions.'

It is fashionable these days to denigrate the Eleven Plus as elitist but the so-called Tripartite system was based upon IQ testing. There was also a chance at 13-plus to transfer between secondary modern, technical and grammar schools.

It is quite probable that some children did not do themselves justice because the Eleven Plus examination was often held in a strange school, a memory which is still clear in the mind of Margaret Hughes of Pendlebury near Manchester.

'My main memory of junior school was sitting an entrance examination for grammar school. We had to go to school on a Saturday morning, taking with us our own pencil and ruler. I don't think we used pen and ink until later. I do remember ink wells set in the tops of the desks.'

I have very close personal links with this system as I began my teaching career at Smithhills Grammar School in Bolton. This was part of an experimental system of new buildings called the Base System, the brain child of the Director of Education named George Selly. He was referred to by the staff as Selly and

The first time out at Nelson on 25th May 1957 for the Darwen Morris Dancers.

the Basemakers as a pun on Gerry and the Pacemakers who were literally in full swing during the 1960s. On a single base three schools were constructed – a secondary modern, a technical and grammar school – and if it was felt that a pupil had been misplaced there was an easy system of transfer.

Apart from normal school the youngsters of the 1940s and the 1950s did not 'have nowt to do'. Many – indeed the majority – went to Sunday school, joined in church processions and enjoyed Scouts, Guides and Boys and Girls Brigades. Ada Hughes of Ashton remembers these times:

'All children, it seemed, went to Sunday school in the 1940s. This was at parents' encouragement though it was rare for them to attend services so I am not sure whether the parents were ensuring that the children had a good, moral upbringing or whether they just wanted a couple of hours to themselves. When I became an adult my mother admitted to me that she and my father looked forward to two uninterrupted hours together in bed on Sundays.

'On Whit Friday there would be the processions behind the tall, colourful banner of each church, the ends of the wooden poles sitting in leather holsters strung round men's waists. The brass bands were always the main attraction for the people who stood on the pavements shaking paper streamers stuck on thin sticks. Roses and union flags were also prevalent and the smell of beer hung heavy on the air as pub doors stood ajar. Catholics who walked on a Whit Sunday hoped it would rain on the "proddy-dogs" Friday but when the weather was good one would hear phrases from "our side" like "the sun shines on the righteous" and the Catholics would say of inclement weather during their walk "God waters his own flowers". Little Italy in Manchester had a very different sort of Whit Walk, very sombre but colourful, the men bearing an effigy of the Virgin Mary through the streets, she looking sad with mounds of lilies around her feet.'

Mabel Mustoe of Rochdale has similar memories but hers were more rurally based.

'Living in a village, life centred round the chapel, and I attended Sunday school from the age of two years along with Ruth. As far as I remember Jack never attended and never joined in any of the activities, but Ruth and I were into everything that went on.

Most mothers made at least some of their children's clothes.

'Living by us was a family of one boy and one girl and Joan who was born just six weeks after me. She contracted polio as a baby and was left with a paralysed leg. She was put into the Crippled Children's Home, where she stayed until she was six, then came home wearing a built up boot and irons on her leg. I immediately took her under my wing, having learned from dad always to have compassion for the unfortunate. Joan remained my friend all through our childhood and we are still in touch some 70 years later.

'Other playmates were five Catholic girls who lived a couple of doors away who seemed to exist on raw onion sandwiches; then there was Eunice who was the daughter of a shop owner, and I was allowed to play with her in their house and huge garden, with tennis court and big lawns and trees to climb. It was Eunice's mum, Mrs Crossley, who taught me how to use a knife and fork – only mum and dad had these at home, us kids made do with a spoon and fingers! Her sister taught us how to make lavender bags and sew beads on cork mats and milk jug covers; we made so many that we had a sale-of-work in their garden and Mrs Crossley made cakes and lemonade and we did a concert on the lawn. Relatives and friends of the Crossleys came and we made £1 10s, which we donated to the home where Joan spent so many years.

'Eunice's life was so different from mine yet we became the best of friends and mum was pleased that I'd got an "up-market" friend. Whatever Eunice was into, mum made sure I could do it too, like dancing class which was beyond mum's means but a word with the teacher and I got to go, paying 9d a week instead of £1 1s a term. Mum would get a drawing of whatever costume was required for our yearly dance display and she would make it for me. Once I was a penguin, once a jockey and of course a ballerina. Dance shoes were a problem as blocked ballet shoes were expensive, but Mrs Crossley came to the rescue with a pair of Eunice's along with a ballet dress which had pink roses on and diamante straps. We had a lot to thank the Crossleys for.

'Joan came to my school and somehow the teachers made me responsible for her. Sometimes this was to my advantage because if Joan had appointments at the clinic or hospital I was always sent with her, so I got out of school each time; if the weather was bad with snow or fog Joan and I were allowed out of school early. She hadn't much of a life – her parents were both drunkards and even though their house was spotless Joan didn't have many pleasures in life. I think my mum did more for her than her own; she shared my toys, and clothes were passed on to her but I wouldn't let her handle my dolls; I loved my dolls and the beautiful clothes mum made for them. I also had a passion for babies and walked nearly all the babies born in the village, the mums seemed to trust me with their offspring.'

All these memories reflect important changes in the social conditions stimulated by the war. The education system was one great improvement and so was the setting up of the National Health Service which will be discussed in the next chapter.

CHAPTER NINE
KEEPING HEALTHY

From the Industrial Revolution onwards few, if any, regions of the world have been as unhealthy as Lancashire. In Victorian times the air was foul and the waters were polluted by chemicals from factories and from sewage produced by unfortunate workers. Manchester was the spawning ground of the Socialist theories of Marx and Engels.

If ever any region needed free health care then it was Lancashire. The polluted atmosphere produced 'unsightly growths' and the Christie Hospital developed to give succour to the afflicted. Christies is still a world famous institution. The atmospheric pollution meant that poisonous smog was an accepted hazard. Brenda Hall has memories of these dismal days and nights.

'It occurs to me while jotting down these thoughts that we now have use of a lot of things which were denied to us when we were young and, more importantly, to our parents, particularly mothers. They it was who had to feed the family during rationing and though we children never went hungry I suspect my mother might have done occasionally. She always put her family first and

Washing was usually done by hand in the days of Dr Lovelace.

Cussons

IMPERIAL 🛡 LEATHER

The Quality Toilet Soap everyone wants!

Some soaps began to promote themselves as luxuries everyone could afford.

that included my father who suffered from bronchitis and emphysema. When we had peasouper fogs in the Fifties she would be worried about him until he returned home in the evening from the factory. She never possessed a washing machine but did all the laundry by hand, squeezing out the water with a mangle. I do not know whether it was lack of money or that you just could not get hold of things like, for instance, toilet rolls (we always used newspaper cut in squares) and sanitary wear (the females of the family using folded cotton squares which had to be washed by hand, dried and re-used). Few people used deodorants, apart from talcum powder.'

Soap was functional rather than sexy and the most famous brands were Wrights Coal Tar, Pears Transparent, Red Carbolic, Lifebuoy and of course the famous Sunlight brands. These were well advertised thanks to the genius of William Hesketh Lever who began life in Bolton and whose initiative eventually became the mighty Unilever organisation.

Having a bathroom and perhaps even a shower with constant hot water literally on tap was also a key to a more healthy lifestyle. Until then there was, of course, the tin bath in front of the fire whilst many town and city dwellers visited the public baths. These had not only a swimming pool but also baths and showers which could be hired. There were also the Turkish baths used by those who needed to steam infection out of their system.

Even toilet papers became more hygiene conscious from the 1950s onwards. First there was the smooth tough Izal, and then softer varieties. Toilet papers were relatively expensive and most schools kept the material in the stationery cupboard, to be obtained on request. Many shy children spent a miserable few hours because they were too embarrassed to ask! Disposable nappies were being planned but had to wait until the end of the Sixties; prior to this disinfectants such as Zal, Dettol and Milton were all needed to sterilise washable nappies and feeding bottles.

No more Nappy Washing

Why wash nappies? Mother and baby benefit so much with

PADDI & PADDI-*pads*

What could be simpler? PADDI, a scientifically designed nappy holder in special soft plastic—*adjustable* for perfect fitting as baby grows; and PADDI-pads—*modern* disposable nappies made from cellulose tissue of surgical quality, faced with cotton wool. Velvet soft and extra-absorbent, PADDI-pads reduce the risk of nappy rash, increase baby's comfort, and are highly recommended by doctors and nurses everywhere. Make a change NOW to PADDI and PADDI-pads—they're the softest and the best, yet they actually cost less.

PADDI garment — Small, Medium and Large sizes—5/6d. each. Extra Large—6/11d. **PADDI-pads**—1/9d. per packet of 10. On sale everywhere.

FOR FREE LEAFLET WRITE TO **ROBINSON & SONS LTD., WHEAT BRIDGE MILLS, CHESTERFIELD**

It is interesting also that it was not until 1946 that a doctor suggested that there might possibly be a link between smoking and lung cancer. Almost everybody smoked and as my own father once remarked to me, 'I smoked more than 30 Senior Service cigarettes a day from the time I started work at 15. Some of my mates smoked Players or Capstan Full Strength and when the

Disposable nappies were only a dream for mothers until the end of the Sixties.

so-called filter tips came in any man who smoked them was considered to be "soft".'

I'll give my father his due –he always advised me against smoking and I never did. I did, however, collect cigarette packets and cigarette cards which was a hobby very popular in the period whilst some also collected match boxes. Jack Carson of Liverpool remembers his collection. 'I used to haunt the docks with my dad who knew lots of Yanks and I could swop Lucky Strike and Camel packets for Gold Flake, Craven 'A', State Express 555, Black Cat, Woodbine and Park Drive. It is funny that everything seemed to be rationed in the war except fags – I still wonder why this was the case.'

Many people who responded to my newspaper and local radio appeals mentioned the reluctance during this period to enter into hire purchase or 'never never' agreements. There was, however, an exception. This was the need to keep the doctor on call and most people made regular weekly

Craven A was just one cigarette that boasted health benefits – the 'rich tobacco, so kind to their throats'.

Capstan cigarettes were promoted as a way 'to make friends'.

payments in the hope that they might never need to call on the medic. Prospective parents also collected weekly sums in order to pay for a midwife and an experienced 'widow woman' to stay with the new mother and child for a day or two.

Most doctors in the 1940s had their own dispensing areas and it was not until the coming of the National Health Service that regular prescriptions were written and delivered to the pharmacist. This evolved into chemists selling a combination of readily available patent medicines and other concoctions only available on prescription.

Lancashire has long been a leader in the production of patent medicines and Beechams pills and powders made in St Helens became world famous. They were sold first on local markets and were so effective that 'for a tanner they were advertised as worth a guinea a box'. Beecham made a fortune and used some of his brass to educate his son who became Sir Thomas Beecham, a colossus in the world of classical music.

Parkinson's Liver and Kidney Pills made in Burnley could be certain to 'cure owt', Stockleys of Accrington made coltsfoot rock which was guaranteed to cure sore throats, Victory V lozenges were made in Nelson and Fishermen's Friends were produced in Fleetwood.

You could purchase syrup of figs, sulphur tablets, Vic vapour rub, Kompo for stomach upsets, the lovely fizzy Andrews liver salts, and Bile Beans which were

We were all Ovaltinies in the 1950s.

A feature of Fisherman's Friend adverts has always been the old type vans parked close to a trawler at Fleetwood Docks.

described as a laxative-plus. What did the plus do, I wonder?

Health shops were a feature as Enid Kemp of Blackburn noted. 'I loved going to Blackburn Market with my brother, and I drank a small sarsaparilla. My brother thought he was very grown up and wicked. He drank a full pint of sarsaparilla beer at the age of 13 and he then smoked half a Woodbine. He was sick – twice!'

The coming of the National Health Service did not and has not replaced patent medicines but it did initially allow people access to free treatment by qualified doctors and dentists. Nowhere was this change of approach more evident than in schools and Doris McDermott of Bury remembered: 'We began to get regular visits from all sorts of medical people in the late 1940s. There were dental and medical inspections, inoculations against polio which alas came too late for some of us. There was great relief to many children when the Salk vaccine impregnated into a sugar lump replaced the injection. And who will ever forget "Nitty Nora the Bug explorer" who looked hard for "nits in our noddle" and helped to cure what had been an on-going problem for more than a lifetime.'

The registration for National Insurance and the Health Service was simplified by keeping the same number as the wartime identity card and then adding other registration numbers as time went on. Many people of course still retain their old wartime number as their medical number.

Eat...

Drink...

Enjoy...

Outspan

ORANGES AND GRAPEFRUIT

Yes, oranges...and grapefruit...but oh, what a difference! Sweet, succulent Outspan Oranges and Grapefruit — the very pick of South Africa's golden crop — simply defy comparison.

The Golden Fruit from SOUTH AFRICA

Such delights as fresh citrus fruits were missing from the diet of many children in the Forties and Fifties.

During and just after the war rationing of food was a health problem especially for young children who suffered from the lack of a regular supply of Vitamin C. Orange juice was severely restricted and a substitute was available in the form of Delrosa Rose Hip Syrup. As a child living on the Lancashire coast in the 1940s our school helped to gather rosehips which were then sent to the Delrosa factory. We collected the hips and brought them to school where they were weighed. We were given one octagonal and usually shiny threepenny piece for each pound. Growing on the seashore were the black (not red) hips of the Burnet rose which are richer in Vitamin C than the common rose hips. I learned where Burnet rose hips grew because I got fourpence for each pound; I was the envy of many friends who were not in on the black fruit market.

Fruit being in short supply, on the occasions when oranges or bananas did turn up, queues developed and these days we do not understand how patient people could be. Mabel Mustoe of Rochdale was one of the patient ones.

'I queued many times for one banana or an orange. The top of the milk was mixed in with the minute butter ration to make it go further. We learned all kinds of tricks in order to live a normal life. We bought rolls of medical lint to make liberty bodices for the children (coupons were needed to buy clothing). I once made a coat out of an air-force blanket and little waistcoats for kids out of washleathers; they were windproof – I wonder if we were the fore-runners of leather-jacket designers!

'We made jellies with gelatine and the occasional free orange juice which the government gave to all kids. We never found a use for the free cod liver oil though!

'Sweets were rationed to 2 ounces a week per person but medicated sweets were off ration at the chemist's and we bought these to make up. Cigarettes were sometimes in short supply and word would spread like wildfire when shops got them in and we would rush to join the queue. Some shops made customers buy a cheap lighter before letting you have 20 cigs. I was lucky as a friend used to nick them out of the Sergeants' Mess stores and bring some home for me, along with chocolate. In the pictures it smelt a bit like a den of iniquity with the amount of Egyptian "Pasha" cigs smoked along with the smell of medicated sweets.'

Taking a look at the advertisements for healthy living in the 1940s and comparing these with those of the 1960s makes fascinating reading and Audrey Heyworth of Oldham made the point clearly: 'In the 1940s the government was telling us to eat healthily and waste nothing. By the 1960s there were all sorts of products to help well fed people to slim. The *Woman's Journal* for November 1960 (cost 2s 6d ie 12p) advertised both Metercal to replace "ordinary meals" or you could cut your calorie count by dissolving Biscoids in your tea instead of sugar. I remember thinking that in the war they rationed sugar and soon they were telling us that sugar was bad for us!'

By far the best way of keeping healthy is to exercise and those active in the period 1939 to 1969 were much better off than the present generation.

Brenda Hall of New Moston recalls that she 'was introduced to a completely new way of spending weekends when a friend took me along to a local scouts' hut where one night a week a youth hostellers' group used to meet. We were invited to go hiking with them one weekend to Derbyshire and we loved it so much that it became our favourite pastime, walking through beautiful countryside, staying at different hostels, meeting young, active people like ourselves.'

Without making a conscious effort the young were active with no television or video games to distract them, as Brenda Hall records: 'We spent most of our time outdoors, the roads being very quiet then with hardly any traffic. We played whip and top, all down the main road, kicking a can all round the side streets, hide and seek, skipping, and ball games; I don't think we ever got bored. When I was six Jack went to work in the factory with Dad so money became a bit better, although I never realised that we were poor as I never wanted for anything — Mum saw to that! Two years later when Ruth was 14 she began work at Crossley's ladies' outfitters.

'Christmas was always wonderful and now I wonder how Mum ever managed it; she would take me to Universal Stores in Manchester and let me pick my main present – a doll's pram, or desk and chair, typewriter, sewing machine, all these things over the years. Also every year there was a Squirrel's Pet Store, a compendium of games, a chocolate smoker's outfit and a sugar pig in my stocking. Ruth used to help Mum fill two stockings and on Christmas Day she would pretend to be as excited as me as she went through her stocking. I always bought Dad a pair of men's suspenders; the bus driver and conductor who drove our village bus, and who made a great fuss of me were not forgotten – the driver got a cigar and the conductor five Woodbines, Mum providing the cash of course!

'Maybe it's true but I can only remember warm sunny days with perhaps the odd wet Sunday when we would stay indoors after Sunday school and read our comics. Then we would knock on the wall to see if the girls next door were ready to swap theirs.

'A lot of our playtime was spent in a field with a stream running through it; the banks were composed of clay so we would make pretend cakes and things from it and lay them on a big stone slab to dry, and then we would play shop. Many happy hours were spent at the "Little Stream" as we referred to it. Our village policeman was always around and we were scared of him with his big bristly moustache. Jack got caught pinching apples from someone's orchard and had to go to court where he was fined five shillings. Dad had to have a morning off work without pay to attend the court, quite an expensive prank; quite different to today's youthful pranks and punishments.'

Despite this healthy exercise people did get ill and until the 1950s very few sophisticated drugs and techniques were available. The Christie Hospital already mentioned in this chapter was pioneering cures for cancer and newly developed drugs, especially penicillin, would have saved many a life and improved the quality of life for all. Brenda Hall has already described the idyllic chapters of her early life but was sad when her father died.

'Alas, when I was about 13 years old Dad started to be ill; I didn't know what it was all about but I remember he had many visits to a clinic and I later learned that he had TB (tuberculosis), probably as a result of his time in the trenches in the First World War. He was advised to go to a home in Grange-over-Sands where they had to sleep outside on a veranda but he refused, and got up to all sorts of tricks to hide things from Mum; he would put weights in his pockets when visiting the clinic so Mum wouldn't know he had lost weight, and, although she tried to build him up with all sorts of rich food and tonics, she would find some of the food wrapped in newspaper and thrown out. He finally became bed-ridden and died.'

The National Health Service also revolutionised the approach to dental treatment. Until the 1950s it was customary to suggest a 'complete clearance under gas' and then to have a set of false teeth specially made once the gums had shrunk. Many perfectly good teeth were extracted, mainly because the pain of having a filling was considered too great to bear. The development of

Taking an X-ray at the Christie Hospital in 1946.

Did you **MACLEAN** your teeth today?

A brilliant exhibition

MACLEANS Peroxide Tooth Paste makes teeth WHITER

And they were probably her own teeth, after the 'complete clearance' fell out of favour.

local anaesthetics allowed many people to live much healthier and satisfying lives.

The key to health has always been exercise, especially but not exclusively, for the young. Lancashire can claim to be the birthplace of many professional sports but it was the groundswell of physical fitness for all which generated this.

Perhaps it was working hard in oppressive conditions which prevented Lancastrians from becoming complacent about the need for exercise in the open air. No wonder that during the period 1939-1969 sport was of paramount importance and followed as ardently as any religion.

CHAPTER TEN

LANCASHIRE SPORT

Whilst the looms of the mills clattered and the iron foundries roared the folk of Lancashire, especially the men, looked forward to a game of football or cricket. At the end of their Saturday morning shift they would head for their local football match.

It should not be forgotten that of the founder members of the Football League most were in Lancashire. There was Blackburn, Bolton, Burnley, Preston, Everton and Accrington soon to be followed by Blackpool, Manchester United, Manchester City, Liverpool, Bury, Oldham and Rochdale. Why did professional football develop in Lancashire? This was because there were large urban populations who would pay good money to watch the best players.

This is why professional Rugby League also developed in the woollen mill towns of Yorkshire and why they fought out matches with teams from the cotton and coal areas of Lancashire. Folk in the county still remember the heroes of Wigan, Widnes, Warrington, Swinton, Salford, Oldham, Rochdale and St Helens.

It was also the reason why Lancashire League cricket could afford to attract the world's best players and continued to do so until the late 1960s. After this time fast air transport and an increasing number of test matches heralded the decline in standards of the league professionals.

Relatively minor sports such as crown green bowling, which is typical of Northern England, Rugby Union, hockey and greyhound racing were also amongst Lancashire's attractions between 1939 and 1969. John Norman of Blackburn pointed out to me that 'few people realise that in the 1950s and

1960s greyhound racing was Britain's most popular sport after football. There were popular tracks at Preston, Blackpool, Blackburn, Bolton and Belle Vue in Manchester.'

Those who write about the hey-day of football and cricket in Lancashire, however, always point out that 1939 was the watershed. The disruptions of war blighted many a career and in 1946-47 when sport again took centre stage the 'gates' around the county were amazing. Bill Shankly, the Liverpool manager, was a player at this time and when he was later asked if football was a war or a religion he replied, 'No – it's more serious than that!'

Let us therefore consider football during and just after the war. Ron Ormerod of Brierfield near Burnley told me of one very amusing event:

OFFICIAL RACE CARD - 78th Meeting - NINEPENCE
Copyright (all rights reserved)

THE STADIUM
ST. ANNES ROAD, BLACKPOOL.
PROPRIETORS:
BLACKPOOL GREYHOUND RACING & SPORTS Co., Ltd.
Under the Rules of and Licensed by
the National Greyhound Racing Club
Secretary: K. BUXTON   Tel.: S.S. 42004

Friday, 26th OCT., 1962
at 7-15 p.m.

| | Stewards: | |
| C. BOTTOMLEY | F. STANLEY | W. H. HARVEY |

Director of Racing:
F. STANLEY

| Ass. Racing Manager: | Kennel Manager: | Paddock Steward |
| K.BUXTON | T. B. WALKER | W. KEOGH |

| Starter: | Timekeeper: | Judge: |
| H. HUGHES | W. T. TURNER | C. BOTTOMLEY |

Veterinary Surgeons:
R. B. HORNBY B V.Sc. M.R.C.V.S.
J. C. MILLER B.V.M.S. M.R.C.V.S.

'Towards the end of the war "guest" players were appearing in football teams. Players' appearances were still controlled by what were called the "exigencies of the Service", meaning whether they could be released from duty for a Saturday afternoon or how far they were allowed to travel. Ironically, one of the guest players for a period at Turf Moor was John Shreeve, the Charlton Athletic full back, who

Greyhound racing was one of the most popular sports in Lancashire.

In 1947 Burnley reached the FA Cup Final, only to be beaten 1-0 by Charlton Athletic.

was to play against Burnley in the FA Cup final of 1946-47.

'A match was due against Sunderland (League North), and in a strange way the fixture produced the unexpected. Burnley had adopted a pre-war strip of white shirts and black shorts with a white stripe down the seam. The Wearsiders arrived at Turf Moor under the impression that their erstwhile Division One opponents were still registered under claret and blue and, to prevent a colour clash with their own red and white stripes, brought a white strip. After a hasty conference Burnley officials dug out a somewhat tattered old-style claret and blue strip. Hence confusion unconsciously further confounded the spectators. As Sunderland were an attraction, many of the 23,000 in attendance were under the impression that the claret and blue team was Burnley and gave their support accordingly – particularly when this side scored!'

Probably the best known quote about the 1946-47 team came from *Daily Express* columnist Henry Rose who, after a particularly poor early season performance against Newport County, dubbed them 'ten comedians and an amateur' (Peter Kippax). In the end, though, these comics quite definitely had the last laugh didn't they?

In the days before the Premier League was ever thought of, Burnley were in the Second Division and in 1947 were promoted to the First Division and reached the final of the FA Cup only to be defeated 1-0 by Charlton Athletic. To reach the final at Wembley, Burnley defeated three First Division sides including Liverpool who finished up as League Champions. How the fixtures were ever completed in 1947 was a mystery because the year was blighted by one of the coldest winters on record. Burnley's promotion year did not end until June!

Thousands of people flocked to watch football and although there was no crowd violence the grounds were not capable of withstanding such numbers. Norman Entwistle told me: 'It was 9th March 1946 at Burnden Park at Bolton that I nearly died. My dad and I only just avoided a crush which killed 33 people and injured more than 500. The game was against Stoke and what I find amazing is that by half past three the dead and injured had been taken away and the game was started. I've written down the official gate as 65,419 but most people who were there think that the gate was closer to 85,000.'

On a happier note one of the most nostalgic Cup Finals ever played was in

1953 when Blackpool beat Bolton Wanderers 4-3. This has been known as the Matthews' final and was the first live game which I ever saw on television. I wanted Blackpool to win in Coronation Year because I loved to watch the Wizard. If the game had been played with present day rules, however, Bolton would have won by a street. Bolton's full back was injured and as no substitutes were allowed the Matthews' genius was allowed full reign and he tore ten-man Bolton apart.

These days it is sad that Accrington are no longer in the Football League proper

Burnden Park, Bolton, 9th March 1946 – 33 fans dead and more than 500 injured.

OFFICIAL   PROGRAMME

THE
BOLTON WANDERERS   Tel. 800
FOOTBALL & ATHLETIC CO., LTD.
President : SIR WILLIAM EDGE, Bart.
Directors :
C. N. Banks *(Chairman)*   Dr. A. Cochrane   P. Duxbury
F. Prestwich   Alderman J. Entwistle, J.P.   W. Hayward
E. Gerrard   H. Warburton
WALTER J. ROWLEY, *Secretary-Manager*
H. ABBOTTS, *Assistant Secretary*

THE F.A. CUP—SIXTH ROUND

Bolton Wanderers

VERSUS

Stoke City

At BURNDEN PARK, BOLTON
Saturday, 9th Mar., 1946

KICK-OFF **3-0 P.M.**   PROGRAMME 1D.

NEXT HOME MATCHES :
WEDNESDAY, MARCH 13th.   Kick-Off **3-0** p.m.
THE FOOTBALL LEAGUE
WANDERERS v. BRADFORD (P.A.)
SATURDAY, MARCH 16th.   Kick-Off **3-0** p.m.
CENTRAL LEAGUE
Wanderers Res. v. Newcastle U. Res.

THE FOOTBALL ASSOCIATION CHALLENGE CUP COMPETITION

FINAL TIE

BLACKBURN ROVERS
v
WOLVERHAMPTON WANDERERS

SATURDAY, MAY 7th, 1960   KICK-OFF 3 p.m.

EMPIRE STADIUM
WEMBLEY

OFFICIAL PROGRAMME   ·   ONE SHILLING

Sadly the Rovers were beaten 3–0 by Wolves.

but the glory days of the club were without doubt the season 1954-55 when they finished runners up in the Third Division (North) but the club was paving the way for the future. Eric Whalley, now the Chairman of the club, remembers this time when, 'Not only was the football good and the crowds comparable with most but Accrington was the very first club to play competitive games under lights on Friday evenings. This meant that local people could watch Stanley on Friday and either Burnley or Blackburn on a Saturday afternoon. You could say that Lancashire began the trend of football being played on every day – or should it be night – of the week. We even had an important sponsor – we all looked forward to a Holland's pie at half time.'

Holland's pies are still made at Baxenden near Accrington and as I write these notes the famous cook Delia Smith, herself a football fan and director of Norwich City, selected Holland's as the 'best football pie in Britain' and visited the bakery to celebrate the fact.

My own memory of that season is watching a friendly floodlit game between Accrington Stanley and St Mirren during the 1954-55 season, wondering if games so illuminated would ever catch on. And yes, the pies were very good!

Another sporting memory for me was being present at Old Trafford in 1956 when England beat Australia in a test match with Jim Laker taking nine wickets in the first innings and all ten in the second. I had borrowed a pair of field glasses and each time a Laker delivery hit the pitch I could see a puff of dust lift from the ground as the ball spun viciously.

These days the Lancashire town soccer teams rejoice at gates in excess of 10,000 but in the 1950s and 1960s the cricket teams in the Lancashire League could often top that figure. They also had their sponsors even at this time and could therefore attract the best players in the world to act as the single professional they were allowed.

Here on Saturday and later Sunday afternoons as well, great players such as Worrel, Weekes and Walcott battered the bowlers to all parts of the ground and occasionally high over the boundary into the local countryside. It was also in the Lancashire League that West Indian fast bowlers first learned to terrify batsmen, including the present author. Here came Charlie Griffiths, Wes Hall and Roy Gilchrist and whilst all these players were feared on the playing field they also became much loved by the local folk.

When I was asked to write a history of Lancashire Cricket League in 1998 I found that many of these West Indians regularly came back to Lancashire to visit old friends.

Although Sir Learie Constantine played in the 1930s he was regarded as an icon in Nelson and when he returned to the town to make a television documentary in 1966 he was afforded a hero's welcome. Learie did more to break down racial barriers in Lancashire than any other person before or since. When Sir Learie was made the first coloured life peer he became Lord Constantine of Maraval (Trinidad) and Nelson!

Sir Learie Constantine returns to Nelson in 1966. The town still loved the famous cricketer some 30 years after he performed wonders on the field.

Constantine's batting record of 192 not out was only beaten by another West Indian in 1949. Everton Weekes made 195 not out against Enfield and Everton returns regularly to Bacup to visit friends and swap cricketing stories.

Everton Weekes, who beat Constantine's batting record in 1949.

Although the Lancashire League, based around the textile towns of East Lancashire, attracted most of the best professionals those who follow the Central Lancashire League based around Rochdale are right to argue that they could also attract the best players in the world, including Garfield Sobers. Taking these two leagues together there was no doubt that during the period 1950 to 1970 the world's very best cricketers performed before large and very appreciative audiences.

Rugby League in the post war period always attracted huge crowds and during this time was my own particular favourite. I love to have long animated conversations with one of the game's historians Nigel Winnard who now lives in Chorley but who spent his formative years in Wigan.

Karel Tom Van Vollenhoven played at St Helens from 1957 to 1968.

'It used to be said in the Fifties', said Nigel with a grin, 'that if you whistled down a Wigan, Leigh or St Helens mineshaft out came a huge prop forward. In those days Rugby League was a winter game. There was nothing like standing on the terraces on a cold wet January afternoon watching steam rise from a mud-stained pack of forwards. League was faster than Union because there were only 13 men instead of 15 in each side and therefore there was more space on the pitch. We always said that League was a professional game but, as you know, it should be described as semi-professional. Players had day jobs which they dare not give up – they trained hard for two nights a week and played on Saturday afternoons. It is hard to list the great players since 1946 when things got going again after the war but some do stand out. There was Billy Boston who was and still is a legend in Wigan and two other great wingers were Brian Bevan of Warrington and the South African policeman Karel Tom Van Vollenhoven who scored 392 tries for St Helens in a playing career which lasted from 1957 to 1968. There was Alex Murphy, a real character of a scrum half, and we do really have to mention a Yorkshireman who was not a player but one of the most famous characters of early television. Eddie Waring put televised Rugby League on the map and his phrase "Up and Under" is still a legend. Eddie even used the phrase when co-presenting *Its a Knockout* with the equally extrovert Stuart Hall. I can't end this chat about Rugby League in Lancashire without referring to your lot in Barrow with the stand off half Willie Horne partnering my old mate Ted Toohey, a scrum half who came from Wigan to join Horne.'

I never tire of talking to Nigel Winnard who in true Lancashire style 'reads much and forgets nowt'.

I mentioned to Nigel one of my favourite Rugby League characters, the Barrow prop forward of the 1940s who was good enough to tour Australia – Ginger Hughes.

'Ah,' mused Nigel, 'there was a tough character. For a while it looked as if his son would become a rugby legend of the 1960s. But instead he went to play football for Blackpool and became such a great full-back that the Seasiders sold him to Liverpool. Emlyn Hughes – Crazy Horse himself – was Captain of Shankly's Liverpool and of England.'

Thinking about great English captains, I have been fortunate enough to interview two of the great Lancashire captains of the Fifties and Sixties in the course of my freelance work with BBC Radio Lancashire.

These are two of the greatest gentlemen that I have ever had the pleasure of talking to – Ronnie Clayton and Jimmy Armfield. Ronnie Clayton, ex Blackburn Rovers and England captain, told me a wonderful story of those days when professional footballers were largely home based, modestly paid and loved the game for its own sake.

'I remember going to Wembley as England captain,' recalled Ronnie Clayton. 'I had no car then – none of us did – and I arranged to meet Stan Matthews, then with Blackpool, and Tom Finney of Preston North End at Preston station. We travelled third class on the train and had to stand most of the way. The train was late and so Stanley Matthews made the decision that we had to take a taxi from Euston to Wembley. When we arrived the manager Walter Winterbottom was angry when Stanley gave him a receipt for 7s 6d (37p) for the taxi fare. Walter snorted that we should have taken either the tube or the bus and would only pay half the bill, which was 3s 9d. I still laugh about that today and wonder what the stars of Manchester United and Arsenal and others would think about that?'

Another magical memory for me during this series which I called *Lancashire Sport*, was when I spoke to Jimmy Armfield in a break while preparing for a game for Radio 5 Live. We talked about his days as Blackpool and England captain. 'We were not pampered much,' he said. 'On home match days I walked from my mother's shop to Bloomfield Road where the gate would eventually top 30,000. If we won I would go home to my tea and then stroll out to meet my friends. If we lost and I had not had a good game I did not risk a roasting but sat at home hoping for an improvement in the next match.'

Clayton, Armfield, Matthews, Finney and Lofthouse are legendary names yet none were paid fortunes but all retained their modesty. Their photographs appeared everywhere but none had agents or were paid vast royalties. Not even their boots were sponsored!

None of these gentlemen (and I mean gentle men) 'went to the dogs' and they looked after their minds and their bodies. They deserve their honoured place in the history of Lancashire. They were men of the people and proud of their towns.

As mentioned at the beginning of this chapter, it came as a surprise to me to learn that greyhound racing was second only to football as a spectator sport during the period 1939-1969. The working man has often been a betting man but the dogs made few rich apart from the bookies.

Old Lancashire also has a firm link with horse racing, with Haydock Park and Aintree still being famous. Until the 1960s, however, Manchester Racecourse on the outskirts of the city at Broughton was a popular venue. I once played cricket nearby and realised that this was once the venue of County Cricket and where I saw a scorebook containing the name of W.G.Grace.

I am sad that the old racecourse has gone but at least Aintree has survived and is still regarded by most as home of the greatest race in the world. Jim Stanway of Liverpool had an uncle who was a 'tic-tac' man who worked Aintree during the 1950s. 'He had a face like a ferret and an eye like a hawk,' Jim told me with a grin, 'he had not been to school in his life and could hardly read or write. He could, however, work out the odds on a winning horse with the speed of a modern computer. He would bet on anything unless he was at work helping other people bet. He was a bookies runner. When betting was illegal he would carry bets between punter and bookmaker. He once said to "a southern toff" that Lancashire invented proper betting. When asked to explain what he meant by "proper" betting he scowled and made the point that Littlewoods and Vernons Football Pools were both Liverpool companies. I once saw him with a friend sitting on a bowling green bench in a Southport park. Guess what they were doing? They were betting on the outcome of a friendly game of bowls between two old ladies in their seventies!'

Crown green bowling to a Lancastrian is both a pastime and a serious sport. 'Professionals' operated during the 1950s, with the prize money offered by the Waterloo Hotel near Blackpool airport being worth going into serious training for.

The 'northern' greens are crowned which means that they slope slightly from the crown of the grass rather than being rolled flat. This requires greater skill, although some critics would say local knowledge, but in any event the game is still highly popular and is played in all weathers.

My father was a mad-keen and good bowler for most of his life. His ethic was work hard, play hard and enjoy life. He envied nobody and this I think was typical of a Lancastrian in this period. Although this chapter has concentrated mostly on professional sport the word 'professional' does not mean the same now as it did in the period 1939-1969.

Then the enjoyment of sport came first and the reward a very poor second. In the words of Ronnie Clayton of Blackburn Rovers football club (a one club man) and England, 'We played because we loved it. Our relatively small wage was then regarded as a bonus.'

What I have loved whilst writing this period of my county's history is the simplicity and honesty of life between 1939 and 1969.

Oh, yes, those were the days!